{POLISHING YOUR PROSE}

POLISHING YOUR PROSE

HOW TO TURN FIRST DRAFTS INTO FINISHED WORK

STEVEN M. CAHN & VICTOR L. CAHN

COLUMBIA UNIVERSITY PRESS · *NEW YORK*

COLUMBIA UNIVERSITY PRESS
Publishers Since 1893
New York   Chichester, West Sussex

cup.columbia.edu
Copyright © 2013 Columbia University Press

Library of Congress Cataloging-in-Publication Data

Cahn, Steven M.
Polishing your prose : how to turn first drafts into finished work / Steven M. Cahn and Victor L. Cahn.
p.   cm.
ISBN 978-0-231-16088-9 (cloth : alk. paper) — ISBN 978-0-231-16089-6
(pbk. : alk. paper) — ISBN 978-0-231-53201-3 (electronic)
1. English language—Rhetoric. 2. Report writing. 3. English language—Style. 4. Editing.
I. Cahn, Victor L. II. Title.

PE1408.C24   2013
808'.042—DC23
2012020433

BOOK DESIGN *by* VIN DANG

TO THE MEMORY OF OUR PARENTS,
EVELYN BAUM CAHN AND JUDAH CAHN

[CONTENTS]

M A R Y   A N N   C A W S

The authors want to have made this book both short and readable: a double bravo. And it is both those things, as well as eminently useful. Before you plunge into reading this "how to" guide, you might well wonder what use it would serve. Even should you be without desire for improvement in your writing—more clarity, more concision, more, well, all sorts of things—you might actually enjoy reading these pages.

I would make the rather peculiar suggestion of starting from the end—peculiar because the tendency in reading whatever kind of document is to start at the beginning. But at the end of this book, Victor L. Cahn's delightful remembering of his confronting the universe of academia is sufficiently wry, condensed, and convincing to persuade you (it does me) that this man knows how to write. Just listen to this:

> Physics. My world. My thing.
>
> Yet would the challenge be sufficient? "Basic Concepts" had a juvenile tone, and I was not interested in mere basics, for I was already involved in relativity.

Nothing is more appealing than obvious arrogance, especially when the author of it is clearly making fun of himself.

That is, among so many other things, what a manual of writing (or anything) necessitates: a sense of humor. Without that, all the suggestions would fall dreadfully flat. Humor serves the purpose of making us feel included in the telling; this is not a sermon but rather a discussion with us, full of helpful illustration. Amazingly, the chosen exemplary sentences — and then paragraphs — seem in every case appropriate to what the authors want to prove. These goals include, for example, removing a drearily inept sentence here, eliminating there a group of words that prove utterly unnecessary, or, elsewhere, inserting a "quite," as in a recognizable quotation from Oscar Wilde:

> To be sure, sometimes an appropriate qualifier helps. Such is the case, for instance, when the writer seeks to be dryly ironic, as in this line from Oscar Wilde's "The Soul of Man Under Socialism":
> "All authority is quite degrading."
> Without "quite," the sentence languishes. With "quite," it clicks.

As someone who finds choosing examples to illustrate grammatical or theoretical points particularly trying, even extraordinarily difficult, let me say how impressive these selections are. Each is exactly, precisely fitting to the point being made.

This is an entirely different talent from that of clarity, although I hasten to say that the Cahn brothers have a fine sense of the clear, and of the harmony of the whole. I wonder if this might have to do with their musical experience: Victor as a violinist, Steven as a pianist. Their ears are trained and so are sensitive to each nuance of each phrase: here too much, here too little, overall the right harmony.

We know that to write well, we have to think well. We also know that one of the best ways to proceed, in writing as in thinking, is to encounter a successful example of the kind of work we would like to undertake and complete. The Cahns are offering here first, a series of strategies, and then, an experiential guide. What I greatly enjoyed, and with some surprise, was, after an intelligent choice of practice sentences and paragraphs, the concluding decision to leave the final working out to the writers themselves. Now they, having read the rest, could go their own way.

Apart from the useful strategies and models of concision and elegance, what we have here is a narrative. As unexpected a gift as anyone could wish for, the storyline moves from advice of the apparently simplest kind (not too many adjectives, no jargon, that sort of thing) to a series of paragraphs and their repeated and repeating alteration. It aims at uncluttering, and is itself uncluttered. The conclusion is a wonderful encomium about unending change: we never stop bettering what we write.

What a grand end to the narrative: that there is no perfect end. There is no finished and final smooth overlay to the work. Thus it continues, and far beyond the student days. This book is about real things, in real time, on the real page. More important still, it is about the real writing mind, in which we absolutely have to have confidence. This book develops confidence, through its completely convincing narrative.

———

Mary Ann Caws, past president of both the Modern Language Association and the American Comparative Literature Association, is distinguished professor of English, French, and comparative literature at The City University of New York Graduate Center.

[ACKNOWLEDGMENTS]

The plan for this book was developed primarily by Steven M. Cahn, and the bulk of the writing was done by Victor L. Cahn. We share equal responsibility for the final product.

We are particularly pleased that Mary Ann Caws has provided a foreword, and deeply appreciate her generous words.

We wish to thank Wendy Lochner, our editor at Columbia University Press, for her support and guidance. We also thank editorial assistant Christine Dunbar, manuscript editor Leslie Kriesel, and other members of the staff of the Press for assistance throughout production.

INTRODUCTION

Here's the situation.

In front of you sits a piece of writing you've just completed. You probably began with several ideas that evolved into a working thesis, which you then supported with argument and evidence. Along the way you may have discovered that your perspective on the subject had changed, and therefore the thesis had to be clarified, modified, or even recast. But you handled this task as well, and thereby unified your thoughts from introduction through conclusion.

Thus the toughest part of the creative process is over. What remains, though, is still a challenge: fine-tuning your product so that it communicates as effectively as possible what you're trying to say.

How do you proceed? How do you take your draft, which you know is better than "rough" but worse than "smooth," and refine it?

This book is intended to help. It's divided into two sections. In the first, we offer ten strategies for correcting an individual sentence. These don't cover every error, but we think they apply to virtually every manuscript. Each strategy is complemented by five practice sentences.

In the second section, we demonstrate how the principles we advocate can be used in editing paragraphs. We also add a few more guidelines.

We don't focus on rules of grammar, such as those about pronoun case or verb mood, nor do we stress subtleties of punctuation. We touch on these matters, but when issues of mechanics arise, here and elsewhere, we advise you to consult a quality reference book. Besides, we want to keep our volume short and readable.

Remember, too, that you may disagree with some of our suggestions. Virtually all edicts about writing have exceptions, and the ultimate measure of your prose is whether it succeeds with your audience.

Perhaps most important, in offering these tips, we don't want you to lose your individual tone. Every writer has a voice, and our goal is that yours will resound with clarity of thought and felicity of style.

We conclude with two samples of our own individual work. After reading so much of our counsel, you deserve to see how we apply it when the material belongs entirely to us.

PART I

STRATEGIES

If we were asked to select the one fault common to most bad writing, our answer would surely be verbosity. Everyone has experienced the frustration of trying to read an article or book in which the author's concepts are stated so wordily or ostentatiously as to blunt their impact. The reality is that fewer and simpler words both create energy and elucidate meaning. Therefore our first three suggestions all concern ways to eliminate prolixity.

1. USE CONCRETE SUBJECTS AND VERBS

Here's a familiar sentence opening:

There is a simple reason for Susan's decision . . .

At once the author is overwriting. Whenever possible, avoid "there is," a flabby construction. Instead we could begin:

A simple reason for Susan's decision is . . .

Here's another example:

There is a book on the table.

Try instead:

A book rests on the table.

The same principle applies to "It is." For instance:

It is often thought that . . .

That convolution may suit Jane Austen (as in the opening line of *Pride and Prejudice*: "It is a truth universally acknowledged . . ."). For our purposes, however, try:

Many readers think that . . .

Or:

Many voters believe that . . .

The tight subject and active verb are more spirited.

Here's another problematic usage:

The fact that he appeared made all the difference.

Ninety-five percent of the time when you write "the fact that," you can cut "the fact." Thus you could offer instead:

That he appeared made all the difference.

Technically, you're taking "that he appeared" and turning it from an adjectival clause modifying "fact" into a noun clause that becomes the subject of the sentence.

Here are other empty constructions that invite tightening:

WEAK	BETTER
for the reason that	because
at that point in time	then
any and all	any *or* all
give consideration to	consider
of the opinion that	think *or* believe
few in number	few
all too often	often
oftentimes	often
serves to inform	informs

ask the question	ask *or* question
at a time when	when
whether or not	whether
may sometimes	may *or* sometimes
give encouragement to	encourage
regardless of the fact that	although
in the event that	if
disappear from view	disappear
encircle around	encircle

The list of such usages is endless, as are the opportunities to eliminate them.

Samples for Correction:

1. Oftentimes he reported on and exposed the fact that in the world of today, stars, celebrities, and other well-known famous people may on certain rare occasions sometimes demand extra special attention and consideration.
2. At that moment in the sequence of events that had occurred in the game thus far, no one could have accurately foreshadowed what was about to happen.
3. No matter how energetic the conclusion of his argument turned out to be in the end, in the final analysis that the Senator reached, his reasoning completely lacked power to convince us with real force of any kind.
4. There is no doubt that those of us who read that kind of book are seeking above all to come across entertainment that in its very core is lighthearted, rather than to find stimulation of the sort that inspires us to think deeply.
5. According to the opinion of many of those who have stated their beliefs, whether or not an opera relates a story that serves to create dramatic tension in the plot is a matter of more than a little but less than a lot of concern.

2. AVOID TOO MANY ADVERBS AND ADJECTIVES

We're speaking of modifiers that may sound attractive, but often add nothing. Here are examples:

young girl
little kitten
positive benefits
mutual agreement
terrible calamity
soaring skyscraper
serious crisis

One popular construction appears in many works of criticism:

Throughout the entire play ...

The writer includes "entire" to increase the authority of the claim, perhaps even to imply that whatever pervades the play will burst its boundaries. But "entire" is unnecessary, and the following version suffices:

Throughout the play ...

What other qualifiers invite cutting? Here are a few:

awfully
highly
mostly
quite
particularly
rather
really
slightly
somewhat
truly
very

We'll add one pet peeve of ours, a modifier that achieves both verbosity and pretension. That word is "terribly" when it is intended to denote praise, as in:

She's a terribly gifted lecturer.

"Gifted" alone does the job.

To be sure, sometimes an appropriate qualifier helps. Such is the case, for instance, when the writer seeks to be dryly ironic, as in this line from Oscar Wilde's "The Soul of Man Under Socialism":

"All authority is quite degrading."

Without "quite," the sentence languishes. With "quite," it clicks.

Our rule, however, stands: try to eliminate superfluous modifiers.

Samples for Correction:

1. A sparkling and cheerfully colored tie can really help to lighten up and brighten the somber tones of a dark black suit.
2. We were all extraordinarily shaken and upset by the awful events of the tragedy that suddenly and unexpectedly took place before we were aware of what had transpired in the vicinity of the environment around us where we were located.
3. She is a totally amazing and wonderfully discerning woman, who never ceases to take us aback and leave us stunned and overwhelmed by her surprising and remarkably perceptive insights into whatever topic happens to be under discussion at the present moment.
4. When the breezy wind is truly blowing hard and really swirling wildly in all directions from off the shore of ocean or sea waters, a golf ball hit in what seems to be a straight direction with unerring and perfect accuracy may still wander off-line hither and yon, back and forth, and every which way across the green fairway of the course.

5. In the midst of wholesale uncertainty, confusion, and disorder, our brave and intrepid scout leader refused to surrender passively to the universal panic displayed by the rest of the members of the squad's populace, and instead maintained a cool demeanor of absolute steady calm and assurance.

3. *AVOID JARGON AND BOMBAST*

We understand that every field has its own terminology, and sometimes technical terms are essential to communication among professionals. Too often, however, important points are buried beneath the barrage of language.

To find examples, we turn to what may seem a surprising source: sports broadcasting, which these days has become a fount of overblown phraseology. For instance:

A football player no longer "fumbles." He now "releases the ball onto the gridiron."

A baseball player no longer "runs fast." He now "possesses excellent foot speed" or "commands superb forward velocity."

A basketball player no longer "jumps high." She now "demonstrates great vertical extension."

Why do otherwise down-to-earth commentators use such palaver? Perhaps they want to imbue their words with pseudo-scientific command. Whatever the reason, writers who use the same strategy rarely succeed.

Samples for Practice (some familiar sayings rewritten):

1. Permit somnolent canines to recline in tranquility.
2. A sparse supply of cognition is a minatory entity.
3. A cascading boulder amasses a vacuity of liverwort.
4. Allow that individual who is divested of iniquity to propel the initial apatite.

5. A plethora of cuisine commanders putrefy the victuals.

4. *AVOID REDUNDANCY*

Thus far we have focused on tightening word usage. Now we do the same with ideas.

Too often when writers want to emphasize a concept, they assume that restating it in different words will help. For example:

> Not only did the speaker's presentation create confusion; it also left his audience bewildered and in a state of uncertainty.

"Create confusion" works well. So does "bewildered." So, for that matter, does "state of uncertainty," as would simply "uncertain."

This example may seem outlandish. Yet how often we read something like:

> Unfortunately, the situation resolved badly.

Or:

> As his lips moved silently, we never heard a sound.

In the first example, "unfortunately" and "resolved badly" are repetitive. In the second example, the same may be said of "silently" and "never heard a sound."

Keep in mind, though, that reaffirming an idea for emphasis may sometimes be helpful. In that case, preface the repetition with a transition so your reader understands that you are proceeding purposefully. Here are examples:

> To reiterate
> Again
> At the risk of repetition
> Once more

Samples for Practice:

1. Her performance apparently failed to move or arouse the people and listeners in the phlegmatic audience, who seemed to offer in return nothing more or less than tepid and lukewarm applause, but otherwise to all visible signs that we could discern remained in a passive and unresponsive stupor.

2. In the world of today's contemporary American society, children and young people alike continue to carry on a desperate search to look for truly authentic modern heroes whom they can look up to with respect and admiration.

3. I am often stunned and taken aback by the vainglorious boasts of athletes who guarantee before a game or contest that no matter what happens during the actual event, they are sure to emerge victorious, and that whatever the outcome of the competition turns out to be, there is no chance that they can possibly come in any lower than first.

4. One question we often ask ourselves about certain people whom we come to know is whether the talents and abilities that they possess and demonstrate with such ease and facility were inborn at birth, or whether these skills and attributes were developed through study, perseverance, and hard work over the course of their lives and experiences.

5. Reading one of Agatha Christie's stories or tales of suspense and mystery usually, in fact, very often leaves me bewildered and totally perplexed because of the incredible number of hints, clues, and red herrings that she purposefully drops carefully but casually into the narrative to confuse and puzzle the readers in her audience so as to lead them astray down the garden path about what the actual outcome of the adventure will or will not be in the end, when everything is tied together and wrapped up neatly in an orderly and clear explanation that reveals the truth of exactly what has just occurred and taken place before our very eyes in the book that we have been reading.

5. USE TRANSITIONS TO
LINK SENTENCES AND IDEAS

Imagine that each sentence of your work is a pearl. Transitions form the string that links those pearls.

Or imagine that each sentence is a short path. Transitions are the signposts that guide your reader on the overall journey.

Or imagine that . . . you get the idea.

Some transitions suggest evidence, of which you can never have too much:

For example
For instance
First (or second or third)
Consider

Some suggest similarity or contrast:

Likewise
Similarly
Furthermore
However
Nevertheless
On the other hand
To the contrary

Some suggest confirmation:

Moreover
In addition
Indeed
Equally important

Some suggest restatement:

In other words
To put the matter differently
In brief

Some suggest conclusion:

Hence
Therefore
In sum
Thus
Consequently

Transitions provide readers with the security of knowing that you are in control of the material. They also help you, the author, because if you can't find an appropriate transition, your ideas may not be as coherent as you presume.

Samples for Practice:

1. I believe that W. C. Fields is the funniest man who has ever lived. *The Bank Dick* and *It's a Gift* are two of my favorite movies. I respect the judgment of anyone who agrees with me. Those who reject this opinion always drop in my estimation.
2. When I go to a party, people always seem to talk about travel or cooking. I know nothing about either subject. I don't say anything. I don't go to parties.
3. Harry loved to watch television. He could watch all day. He could simply sit and stare at that box. His business associate, Sam, had no patience for such wasting of time. He actually did the work.
4. Romeo rarely thinks before he acts or talks. He races from one situation to another. He never has a plan that he follows. He is not nearly as intelligent as Juliet.
5. When you learn to drive, you have to keep a lot of rules in mind. You have to drive defensively and watch out for mistakes that other drivers might make. You have to be careful of pedestrians who don't look where they're walking. Too many beginning drivers are concerned only with getting there fast.

6. VARY SENTENCE STRUCTURE

All of us have heard speakers who talk in a monotone or relentless rhythm. Their ideas may be interesting, but the dull presentation crushes audience response. The same phenomenon occurs in writing.

We're not speaking of suspense fiction, where short, terse sentences may create tension:

> He walked up the stairs. The floor creaked. He felt for the doorknob.
> It was cold. He turned it. The door slowly opened.
>> The light revealed a sight too horrible for words.

In nonfiction, however, such style becomes numbing, so you want to vary your tone. For instance, you may write:

> We arrived at the lake early, and the fish were already jumping.

The example contains two coordinate clauses, a legitimate structure, but the combination of a subordinate clause and a main clause may be an intriguing variation:

> When we arrived at the lake early, the fish were already jumping.

Sometimes an introductory phrase works:

> Arriving early, we saw that the fish were already jumping.

Or an unexpected question:

> We arrived at six in the morning. What would we do first?

You can also combine sentences to make the construction longer:

> When we arrived early, the fish were already jumping, so we took out our rods, scurried into the boat, and began the serious work of the day.

In lengthening, however, beware of running on forever:

> What we noticed first when we arrived was the fish, already jumping, leaping, so near our boat that we, free from the pressures of the

workaday world, yet not without care, but somehow with unbridled enthusiasm, itself always tempered by knowledge of the transience of the day, and of time alone, in contrast with the permanence of the lake and the sun beaming overhead, could not help but be reminded of the wonders of existence that never ceased to accompany any journey of this magnitude, especially one taken in conjunction with the special joy to be savored in the presence of this rare company that included not only the three familiar members of our party but also the two guests, each of whom brought a distinctive, not to say singular, aptitude for the adventure at hand, which we would long remember as one of the highlights of the all-too-brief portion of eternity that would be forever known as "the weekend."

The sentence is grammatically proper, but hopelessly convoluted. Such a construction may work for Hegel or Henry James, but not for the rest of us. When you find this sort of monstrosity in your prose, divide it into shorter sentences.

Good writing is like good music. Each is founded on melody and rhythm, and as writers we want to infuse our prose with both.

Samples for Practice:

1. We drove to the park, and we took the roller coaster, and we rode in the bumper cars, and we boarded the Ferris wheel, and we became sick.
2. We always study for exams together. We try to push each other to do our best. We usually do well. Sometimes we don't.
3. The car had been sitting on the road for three days. No one claimed it. Finally someone did. A man said it was his. The man was a stranger in town.
4. Dr. Finnegan, who works in his office on Piedmont Avenue, was born and educated in Ohio, but he has practiced in New York for eight years, and one day he hopes to return to Ohio.
5. The dish that he dropped came from a collection he bought at a time when he was on vacation from a job from which he was fired before he went to school to begin a new career as a caterer.

7. USE PARALLEL STRUCTURES FOR COORDINATE ELEMENTS

Consider this sentence:

He prefers table tennis, chess, and to play golf.

In his sequence of activities, the writer starts to build a pattern of three nouns, but abandons it by changing the last to an infinitive. The sentence therefore lacks parallelism. Here's one solution:

He prefers table tennis, chess, and golf.

Here's another:

He prefers to play table tennis, chess, and golf.

The same principle applies to correlatives, such as "not only . . . but also" and "either . . . or," as in this ill-conceived creation:

She is not only a fine teacher, but also her scholarship shows promise.

Whatever construction follows "not only" should follow "but also." In this case, "not only" is succeeded by a noun and an adjective, so the same pattern should follow "but also":

She is not only a fine teacher but also a promising scholar.

Consider another sentence that lacks parallelism:

His plans include hauling boxes, bags, and buying mops.

One way to rewrite is to include an additional verb:

His plans include hauling boxes, tossing trash, and buying mops.

In this version all three objects of "include" are participle-noun combinations. We could also cut one verb, and allow the first to control three parallel objects:

His plans include using boxes, bags, and mops.

If we want additional parallelism, we could change "mops" to "brooms," and thereby have three playful alliterative "b" sounds: "boxes, bags, and brooms."

On second thought, maybe not.

Samples for Practice:

1. A great work of art moves us not only emotionally but also provokes ideas.
2. The dedicated mail carrier will not be stopped by either rain, sleet, or in snowy weather.
3. Try to write a scary story with a good plot twist and that does not run more than 250 words.
4. He used his computer to write, to research, and for playing games.
5. His greatest pleasure was not performing as a soloist, but chamber music.

8. *PLACE MODIFIERS PROPERLY*

Whether the modifier is a phrase or a single word, improper placement may leave a reader confused. For instance:

> The professor described an earthquake in the midst of her presentation.

Did the earthquake take place during the lecture? Or was the professor recounting an earlier event? The revision should probably read:

> In the midst of the professor's presentation, she described an earthquake.

Here's another:

> Exiting the theater frequently annoys the actors.

Is the writer suggesting that frequent departures prove annoying, or that any single departure is usually an annoyance? Here's one rewrite:

> Frequent exits from the theater annoy the actors.

In other words, when members of the audience constantly rise from their seats, the actors become peeved.

We cannot omit the most famous misplaced modifier of all time, the one uttered by Groucho Marx as Captain Spaulding in the movie *Animal Crackers*:

> One morning I shot an elephant in my pajamas. How he got in my pajamas I'll never know.

Another modifier that creates confusion is "only." Here's one example:

> He would only work in three more films.

As the sentence stands, one possible reading is that the sole employment the actor sought was work in three more films. Another is that he worked in those films, but had nothing more to do with them. Yet what the writer probably means is that this actor's career dwindled to three final performances. Therefore the sentence should read:

> He would work in only three more films.

Here's an additional example:

> Only Andy is twelve years old.

The sentence implies that among a certain group of young people, everyone is older or younger than Andy. He is the sole individual who happens to be twelve.

Now let's shift "only" to another part of the sentence:

> Andy is only twelve years old.

The meaning now is that Andy is unexpectedly young.

Consider the first of two sentences in which the word "nearly" holds sway:

He nearly lost fifty dollars.

In other words, the money was recovered, but barely in time. Here's another placement:

He lost nearly fifty dollars.

The sentence now suggests that he lost perhaps forty-eight or forty-nine dollars.

Here are other words that require careful placement:

almost
even
just
ever
simply

One particularly egregious misplaced element is the dangling modifier, as demonstrated in this announcement played regularly at a train station we frequent:

When purchasing tickets, proper identification is required.

"Proper identification" does not buy tickets. One day we hope to hear another version that clarifies the meaning:

When purchasing tickets, passengers must have proper identification.

Or:

Anyone purchasing tickets must have proper identification.

Here's another example of a dangling modifier:

As a manager, it's important to keep my players alert at all times.

"It" is not the manager. Nor would this rewrite help:

As a manager, my job is to keep my players alert at all times.

"My job" is not the manager, either. One possible rewrite:

As a manager, I try to keep my players alert at all times.

One last error:

> While an undergraduate, Shakespeare became my favorite writer.

For all his accomplishments, Shakespeare never attended college. One possible revision:

> When I was an undergraduate, Shakespeare became my favorite writer.

Samples for Practice:

1. One week after returning from Europe, her daughter was born.
2. Upon entering the doctor's office, the skeleton seemed to jump out at me.
3. Reading a book of instructions occasionally can be enlightening.
4. The demands of two jobs, because of the pressures involved, may prove dispiriting.
5. The boat was sold by a gentleman with a battered hull.

9. *PLACE THE MOST DRAMATIC MATERIAL AT THE END OF SENTENCES*

Let your sentences build. Place introductory clauses and phrases early, and leave the most important words until the end. For example:

> I turned on the light when I entered the room.

The end of the sentence droops. Now let's put the subordinate clause first:

> When I entered the room, I turned on the light.

The sentence concludes with the crucial idea and the most important word. Here's another:

> The candidate worked hard to win over voters during the final days of the campaign.

Now let's switch placement of clauses:

> During the final days of the campaign, the candidate worked hard to win over voters.

This sentence ends with an upsurge.

Sometimes you have to decide which of your ideas is more important, as in this sentence:

> Although he won the golf tournament by six strokes, he had trained for just a few weeks.

This construction implies that the point of greater interest is the player's minimal training, but such is probably not the case. We'd revise the sentence as follows:

> Although he had trained for just a few weeks, he won the golf tournament by six strokes.

This version has a natural upward tone, and therefore the emphasis is on winning, not training. Here's a last example:

> I recently completed a paper concerning imagery in the poetry of Wordsworth for my senior seminar.

The notion that the writer composed the essay for the seminar is secondary, and should not conclude the sentence. Let's try another version:

> I recently completed a paper for my senior seminar concerning imagery in the poetry of Wordsworth.

This revision doesn't work either, because as the sentence is written, "imagery in the poetry of Wordsworth" could be the subject of the entire seminar. Therefore we try again:

> I recently completed for my senior seminar a paper concerning imagery in the poetry of Wordsworth.

The meaning is now clear, but the construction feels convoluted, so we offer one more solution:

> For my senior seminar, I recently completed a paper concerning imagery in the poetry of Wordsworth.

This sentence has both clarity and drama, and is therefore preferable.

Samples for Revision:

1. I was struck by the incredible reverberations, although the lights flashed, too.
2. My terrific meal included the most delicious piece of salmon I have ever tasted, plus a salad and berries.
3. Who cares how he dresses if he can fix the television?
4. When I buy an extra-large popcorn, I don't care where we sit if the movie starts on time.
5. I raced to the front of the room, seizing the moment.

10. MAKE SURE THAT EVERY PRONOUN HAS A CLEAR ANTECEDENT

A pronoun is supposed to take the place of a noun, and your reader should understand exactly which noun is being replaced. For example:

> I visited the library, then purchased a bagel and a cup of coffee. That was what I needed.

As the sentence is written, the reader cannot be certain whether "that" refers to the visit to the library, the bagel, or the cup of coffee. To clarify, you have a couple of options.

Suppose you want to suggest that the whole experience was necessary. You could change "that" from a pronoun to an adjective, then add a noun that encompasses the totality of the adventure:

> That interlude was what I needed.

You could also use "here" instead of a pronoun:

> Here was what I needed.

You could also specify which of the three items was so appreciated:

> That bagel was what I needed.

> The same rule applies to "which," "this," and "it." For instance:

> He took on the most difficult challenge, which freed the rest of us to concentrate on our own tasks.

Instead try:

> He took on the most difficult challenge, freeing the rest of us to concentrate on our own tasks.

Another example:

> This is a question that still puzzles us.

A better version would be:

> This question still puzzles us.

Finally:

> She turned on her computer, downloaded the essay, and started her work. She did it every morning.

To avoid the vague pronoun reference, try:

> She turned on her computer, downloaded the essay, and started her work, as she did every morning.

"As" incorporates the complete ritual. Here's another solution:

> She turned on her computer, downloaded the essay, and started her work, a routine she followed every morning.

When determining whether an antecedent is clear, remember that a pronoun usually refers to the last noun preceding it. Consider this case:

Marilyn gave Margaret a clock that she loved.

Technically, "she" refers to Margaret, but the reader cannot be certain whether Marilyn bestowed upon Margaret a clock that Marilyn treasured, or if the gift itself thrilled Margaret. Let's revise the sentence this way:

Marilyn gave the clock that she loved to Margaret.

We could also reverse the meaning.

Margaret loved the clock that Marilyn gave her.

Whenever you use a pronoun, you should be able to point directly to its antecedent.

Samples for Revision:

1. In our textbook, it gives three rules for diagramming sentences.
2. Crusher and Rocky fought to a titanic draw, and he never recovered.
3. After working for six months in a law firm, I decided to become one.
4. He had to empty all the wastepaper baskets, which was not how he intended to spend his day off.
5. The club will sell tickets for the New Year's Eve party that they hold every year.

PART II

PASSAGES

Now that we've proposed ten strategies for editing, and you've tried to apply them to various sentences, let's consider some larger blocks for revision. We've selected three substantial paragraphs, all taken from a single contribution to a book of essays. The author was a celebrated professor of mathematics, who in the piece under study reflects on the values he acquired and the lessons he learned during his long teaching career. He offers a wealth of intriguing ideas, but as he himself has acknowledged, he is a less than gifted writer. After extensive emendation, the work was eventually published, but for this book he granted us permission to use excerpts from an early draft. In rewriting, we shall strive to maintain his ideas while presenting them more clearly and gracefully.

As you approach each part of this section, we suggest that you first read the paragraph in question, then attempt to improve it. After you've done what you can, turn to our version and see how it compares to yours.

A. THE FIRST PARAGRAPH

This first paragraph appears early in the essay, and we think of it as the author's way to introduce some of the concepts he has percolating.

It is important to recognize the fact that every subject, given that its content is not totally reducible to some other subject area, presents a special set of pedagogic problems arising as a result of the distinctive character of their contents and their essential nature. The problems may be regarded as particularizations of the general pedagogical considerations which must be treated by any and all teachers who seek to seriously discharge his or her educational responsibilities in a highly efficacious manner. The teaching relation is an excessively complex one, and its complexity is readily apparent when one attempts to dissect the relation in order to isolate its component elements. The relation involves the teacher, the material, the student, and the amount of possible instructional methods, all considered within the framework of a particular institution at a given time embedded within a particular social context. No single constituent can be stressed at the expense of the others. No element can be ignored without a loss in quality of the total process. The problem of inadequate teaching should be shared equally by the administration. The reason is because of the policy of college and university administrators which rewards to faculty members promotion and tenure primarily on the basis of each member's research and publication. Those who work actively outside the confines of the classroom have been encouraged to concentrate at the expense of those who would otherwise energetically dedicate themselves to their teaching duties. I am not forwarding the fallacious tenet that teaching skills and the interest and the ability to carry on significant research are mutually exclusive. But in analyzing the teaching situation on the college level, the upshot is that all too often the student and his interests, attitudes, needs, and problems are only given cursory consideration by those involved in structuring and presenting a course. In my opinion, such factors are crucial to the development of a sound educational experience.

Where to begin?

What strikes us first is the author's wordiness. As we suggested, his ideas may be worthwhile, but they are undercut by overwhelming verbosity as well as by a host of other problems. The best way to proceed is one sentence at a time.

Let's start with the first:

> It is important to recognize the fact that every subject, given that its content is not totally reducible to some other subject area, presents a special set of pedagogic problems arising as a result of the distinctive character of their contents and their essential nature.

The opening construction ("It is important to recognize the fact that . . .") is overwritten. Therefore our initial step, in accordance with one of our ten principles, is to cut "the fact." The phrase now reads: "It is important to recognize that . . ."

Better, but can we cut more? How about "It is"?

Earlier we advised avoiding this usage, and here is an ideal opportunity to excise it. But why not go further? After all, these opening words merely alert us to an "important" thought. Why not eliminate the warning and simply state that thought?

The sentence now begins "Every subject."

How about the next phrase: "given that its content is not totally reducible to some other subject area"?

First, the adverb "totally" can be cut with no damage. Either something is "reducible" or it isn't.

How about "area"? Can we distinguish between a "subject" and a "subject area"?

Not easily. Let's remove "area."

Now think about the entire construction that begins "given. . . ." What precisely does it mean?

To be honest, we're not sure. After all, isn't every subject part of another subject?

Therefore we ask whether the phrase "given that its content is not totally reducible to some other subject area" contributes anything at all.

Our answer: no.

Our solution: cut it.

Now just two words of text remain: "Every subject."

Thus we move to the next phrase: "presents a special set of pedagogic problems."

The idea is important, but do we need "special"? Our author is discussing "problems," and aren't all problems in some respect special? In other words, no problems are special. Therefore we need not say more.

Then how about "a . . . set of"? Why "a set of pedagogic problems" rather than just "pedagogic problems"?

No reason.

Now only three words of this adjectival phrase remain: "presents pedagogic problems." We place these after our opening two words, so that the first sentence reads:

> Every subject presents pedagogic problems.

Not bad, but it's flat, so we might want to add a modifier. Before we do, however, we note that the author has added a supplementary phrase of his own:

> arising as a result of the distinctive character of their contents and their essential nature.

In evaluating this thought, we see first that "as a result of" is wordy. Instead we could use "from."

Do we need the adjective "distinctive" before "character"? Probably not.

To what word does the adjectival pronoun "their" refer? "Subject." But "subject" is singular, and "their" is plural. Thus we must twice change "their" to "its."

Notice, by the way, the spelling of "its." We don't use "it's," the contraction of "it is." We also don't use "its'," which doesn't exist. We use "its," the possessive of "it."

We move on. Do we need "essential" to modify "nature"? No.

What is the difference between "contents" and "nature"? We're not sure, so one of the two words can go. "Nature" seems more interesting, so let's keep it.

Now the phrase reads: "arising from the character of its nature."

Yet the construction remains redundant, because "character" and "nature" are virtually synonymous. Of the two, "nature" is again the more interesting, so let's do away with "the character of."

The phrase now reads "arising from its nature."

At this stage, having exerted so much effort to tighten the phrase, we must ask a painful question: what does the phrase "arising from its nature" contribute?

Reluctantly, we answer, "Nothing." Why? Because everything has a "nature." Why specify this particular "nature"?

No reason, we decide. Thus the entire clause, even the pared-down version, may disappear.

Here, then, is the new opening sentence:

Every subject presents pedagogic problems.

But as we noted earlier, this construction sounds flat. How about adding "its own" before "problems"? That insertion suggests that all subjects present challenges, but mathematics, the chief concern of this essay, has unique ones.

At last our tentative version of the opening sentence reads:

Every subject presents its own pedagogic problems.

It's short, direct, and clear: an ideal topic sentence for this paragraph. The implication is that the rest of the paragraph will amplify the nature of those problems, and such is exactly what happens.

After drawing a breath, we move to the next sentence:

The problems may be regarded as particularizations of the general pedagogical considerations which must be treated by any and all teachers who seek to seriously discharge his or her educational responsibilities in a highly efficacious manner.

Some potential alterations are obvious.

"Any and all" can be reduced to "all."

The pronouns "his or her" refer to "teachers" and therefore should be "their."

The adverb "seriously" splits the infinitive "to discharge," rarely a good idea, but the adverb is also superfluous, so we can omit it.

Finally, the adverb-adjective combination "highly efficacious" could be simply "efficacious." For that matter, "in a highly efficacious manner" could be "efficaciously."

Still, we must wonder if these cosmetic changes help. Or do they avoid a larger problem?

To decide, we ask: what does the author seek to say? His sentence implies that the special problems created by mathematics, those mentioned in the previous sentence, are related to general challenges encountered by all teachers, particularly those who are dedicated.

But aren't all teachers supposed to be dedicated? Certainly the ones who might bother to read our author's essay would be.

And aren't these same teachers aware that their profession poses challenges? Absolutely.

Then what does this sentence add? Nothing. It merely reaffirms the concept that teaching offers many problems.

Thus we can cut the entire construction, a move that leaves us once again with our first sentence:

Every subject presents its own pedagogic problems.

We may seem to have accomplished little, but in fact we've cut several dozen words.

Heartened by such progress, we move on:

The teaching relation is an excessively complex one, and its complexity is readily apparent when one attempts to dissect the relation in order to isolate its component elements.

What is "the teaching relation"? Does the author mean the classroom dynamic between teachers and students? Probably. But given his topic, he could also mean the relationship between teacher and subject. Let's assume, however, that he means the former. Can we cut anything?

Consider the first clause: "The teaching relation is an excessively complex one." It may be "complex," but is it "excessively complex?" Is it too complex to be analyzed? No. Thus "excessively" can go.

Now the phrase reads "is a complex one." Why not say simply that the relation is "complex"?

We move to the next clause.

and its complexity is readily apparent when one attempts to dissect the relation in order to isolate its component parts.

This construction, too, is wordy.

What can we cut? How about "readily"? Fine.

What about "attempts to dissect"? We don't intend to fail in our dissection, so we're going to do more than attempt to dissect. We're actually going to dissect. Then let's cut "attempts to."

We can also cut "in order" and leave "to."

But wait: what does the word "dissect" mean? The action involves dividing the object of inquiry into parts. Then what does "to isolate its component parts" add? Nothing. Let's cut that phrase, too.

An aside. The author has written "when one attempts." We don't advocate using "one," a word that sometimes oozes pomposity. We also don't favor "he or she," or any variation such as "s/he." Such usages divert attention from the ideas and instead highlight the artifice of the writing. Therefore when we want to remain gender-neutral, we prefer plural subjects, so the pronoun becomes "they." We also like to use "we," which embraces both writer and audience, and therefore seems inviting. When we speak directly to the reader, we use "you." And when the identity of the author matters, rather than just the ideas themselves, we use "I."

Back to the sentence in question. Here's what we've left ourselves:

> The teaching relation is complex, and its complexity is apparent when we dissect the relation.

At this point we ask: does the author subsequently list what he calls "the component parts" of "the teaching relation"? He does. Well, if he's going to list them, why bother announcing his intention? And why precede that catalog with a caution about its "complexity"? Let us decide for ourselves how "complex" the "relation" is.

In other words, why not drop the whole sentence?

We can't think of a reason.

We've taken a long route to arrive at this conclusion, but the trip was useful. We cut and cut, until we realized that the entire concept was unnecessary. Such a discovery often occurs late in the revision process, and the key is remaining alert for it.

Now where are we? We've reworked a quarter of the original paragraph, and all we have is our first sentence:

> Every subject presents its own pedagogic problems.

With spirits high, we continue:

> The relation involves the teacher, the material, the student, and the amount of possible instructional methods, all considered within the framework of a particular institution at a given time embedded within a particular social context.

Here we learn new information: the ingredients of what the author calls "the teaching relation." But doesn't he mean simply "teaching"? Yes.

Thus let's rewrite the first clause: "Teaching involves the teacher . . ." We note an unwieldy repetition, so we want a synonym for "teacher."

How about "professor"? The word fits, but our author is also speaking of teaching outside the college level.

What about "instructor"? It works better, because it applies to anyone who teaches any subject at any level. We return to the sentence:

> Teaching involves the instructor, the material, the student, and the amount of possible instructional methods.

Here the author misses an excellent opportunity to give his piece style. First he builds a rhythm: "the instructor, the material, the student." Article, noun; article, noun; article, noun. But then he diverges with: "and the amount of possible instructional methods."

We note as well that "amount" is used improperly. The author means "number," which is correct when we are actually counting. "Amount" refers to a single quantity. Thus "the amount of sugar," but "the number of sugar cubes." We also remind our friends in sports broadcasting that they should never say "the amount of points."

The same principle applies to "fewer" and "less," e.g., "fewer laughs" vs. "less laughter."

But leave aside that confusion. Shouldn't we maintain the author's beat by using another article-noun combination? Yes. Can we find one? Well, he's discussing "methods." How about "method"?

Now the sentence reads:

> Teaching involves the instructor, the material, the student, and the method . . .

It's better, but are the four elements in proper order? We don't think so. First, "instructor" and "student" belong next to each other. Second, "material" and "method" both begin with *m*, and in tandem create an effective alliteration. Therefore let's shift the items:

> Teaching involves the instructor, the student, the material, and the method . . .

Sounds good. Now for the second half of the sentence:

> all considered within the framework of a particular institution at a given time embedded within a particular social context.

We note first the repetition of "particular." Can we cut one usage? Yes. How about both? Yes, again.

How about "given?" Would "a time" alone work? Yes, so let's cut "given."

Still, the construction is wordy, so we examine the second part, which includes "institution," "time," and "social context." Can we find a single word that incorporates all three?

We can: "environment," which encompasses everything our author describes.

Now let's go back to the sentence and insert our alternative:

> all considered within the framework of the environment.

We see improvement, but in the first portion of the sentence the author has created a sequence of four words: "instructor," "student," "material," and "method." Should we therefore cut "all considered within the framework of" and make "environment" the fifth in a row? Let's try:

> Teaching involves the instructor, the student, the material, the method, and the environment.

We should. Now let's review what we've concocted:

> Every subject presents its own pedagogic problems. Teaching involves the instructor, the student, the material, the method, and the environment.

The passage is neat, but it feels choppy, so we have to link these two sentences with a transitional word or phrase. Before we try, however, let's ask: what is the author's point? We think he wants to suggest that whatever the specific subject and its problems, teaching always involves these five elements.

And right in that answer we find our transitional idea. Some imagination is needed, but not much:

> Every subject presents its own pedagogic problems. Yet whatever the topic, teaching always involves the instructor, the student, the material, the method, and the environment.

We're now in reasonable shape, at least as far as the first two sentences are concerned. When the author places them in the context of the entire essay, further revision may be necessary, but for the time being, let's move on.

> No single constituent can be stressed at the expense of the others. No element can be ignored without a loss in quality of the total process.

We face a choice. Both sentences are brisk, but they say essentially the same thing. Thus we want to cut.

Before doing so, though, we note the word "constituent." Is it appropriate? It usually signifies a "voter" or a "member of a party." Perhaps the author's other word, "element," would work better.

We also note the verb "can" in the first sentence. Does the author really mean "can"? After all, the truth is that any element *can* be favored. Perhaps he means "should."

Yet in the next sentence "can" works, because the author speaks of the consequences of neglecting one element or another, and how lack of consideration of one element "can" create trouble.

Finally, the author's phrase "No single constituent can be stressed" invokes the passive voice, in which the subject receives the action of the verb. We generally prefer the active voice, in which the subject performs the action: "Stressing one element . . ."

But then what about the verb? If we used this new active construction, would "can" or "should" be preferable?

Neither is ideal, for "can" implies *possibility* or *ability*, while "should" has overtones of *morality*. We want a word that denotes *likelihood*.

How about "could"? Let's see how the new version reads:

Stressing one element at the expense of others could . . .

The result is promising, but now we need a verb to articulate what such "stressing" will do. To that end, we want a word meaning "to cause." How about "cause" itself?

That decision leads to our next question. According to the author, what exactly will be caused? "[A] loss in quality of the total process."

But wait. That "result" is a consequence of *neglecting* one element, not "stressing one element at the expense of others." Therefore let's change the verb, cut the remaining words in the phrase, and replace "could" with "will" to accentuate the almost certain consequences.

Neglecting one element will cause a loss in quality.

Better, but can we compress our verb and object? Can we find a single word to mean "cause a loss in quality"? How about "harm?"

Neglecting one element will harm the total process.

The adjective "total" is unnecessary, so let's cut that. But we also want to clarify that all these elements have importance, and a well-placed modifier might add energy. How about putting "any" before "one"?

> Neglecting any one element will harm the process.

We could cut "one," but we think it adds dramatic emphasis.

Either way, we've made more progress, so let's review what we have thus far:

> Every subject presents its own pedagogic problems. Yet whatever the topic, teaching always involves the instructor, the student, the material, the method, and the environment. Neglecting any one element will harm the process.

Good, but we feel choppiness between the second and third sentences. Can we combine them?

> Yet whatever the topic, teaching always involves the instructor, the student, the material, the methods, and the environment, and neglecting any one element will harm the process.

Earlier we cut "total," but now, just as we have the adjective "one" modifying "element" and helping to maintain parallel structure, so we might like an adjective modifying "process." "Entire" sounds appropriately elevated.

At last our first two sentences read:

> Every subject presents its own pedagogic problems. Yet whatever the topic, teaching always involves the instructor, the student, the material, the method, and the environment, and neglecting any one element will harm the entire process.

The result is brisk and clear. We're now better than halfway through the paragraph.

What's next?

> The problem of inadequate teaching should be shared equally by the administration. The reason is because of the policy of college and university administrators which rewards to faculty members promotion and tenure primarily on the basis of each member's research and publication.

The first error that strikes us rests in the second sentence: "The reason is because." That construction is intrinsically repetitive. We should use either "The reason is that" or "because" but not both. Here we can change the expression to read: "The reason is that the policy of . . ." or "by the administration, because the policy of . . ."

But this error is minor in comparison with a larger transgression: lack of paragraph unity. Until now, the author has targeted qualities in teaching, and he will soon resume that task. For a moment, though, he loses focus and assigns blame for a crisis he has yet to describe. Here, then, we can establish a supplementary principle:

Maintain unified paragraphs

A paragraph should have a topic sentence, and all details in the paragraph should support that sentence.

How do we resolve this specific situation? We have two choices. The first is to expand the topic sentence so that it incorporates the second theme. What is the topic sentence for this paragraph? The first: "Every subject presents its own pedagogic problems." Can we expand this sentence to include the theme of administrative neglect or interference?

No.

Thus we must follow the second alternative: to eliminate all material about administrative policy from this paragraph and save the concept until later.

With that strategy in mind, let's proceed sentence by sentence.

The problem of inadequate teaching should be shared equally by the administration.

Is this sentiment relevant? Eventually it may fit into the essay, but it doesn't belong here, so let's drop it for now.

The reason is because of the policy of college and university administrators which rewards to faculty members promotion and tenure primarily on the basis of each member's research and publication.

We've already considered the faulty opening construction. More important, the thought itself doesn't work here, so let's remove this one, too.

> Those who work actively outside the confines of the classroom have been encouraged to concentrate at the expense of those who would otherwise energetically dedicate themselves to their teaching duties.

Three small errors come to our attention.

The first is the phrase "confines of the classroom." It connotes that the classroom is like a prison, not the most generous of thoughts. Thus "confines of the" should be cut.

Second, "energetically dedicate" is redundant, so the adverb "energetically" can be omitted.

Finally, the four-word phrase "to their teaching duties" is overdone. How about simply "to teaching"?

All these corrections help, but they do not eliminate the crucial problem with this sentence: it, too, is out of place. Let's put it aside. We move on:

> I am not forwarding the fallacious tenet that teaching skills and interest and the ability to carry on significant research are mutually exclusive.

First, the author uses "forwarding" incorrectly. What he means is "proposing." We're also not pleased with "fallacious tenet." "Fallacious" should be applied only to an argument, not a tenet. Our author should have used "false," which may describe a statement. In addition, "tenet" implies something worth believing, but our author clearly disagrees with the notion in question, so "assertion" might be better.

Yet despite these trifling adjustments, the overall construction remains wordy. Before we devote time to trimming it, though, we recognize that the concept itself is intrusive. True, the balance between the demands of research and teaching may need to be considered, but this paragraph is not the place. Thus we cut the whole sentence.

What's next?

> But in analyzing the teaching situation on the college level, the up-
> shot is that all too often the student and his interests, attitudes,
> needs, and problems are only given cursory consideration by those
> involved in structuring and presenting a course.

Now the author has recovered his footing. Indeed, the conjunction "But" indicates that he understands that he has wandered and
is trying to redirect our attention to the subject of this paragraph.

What about the sentence itself?

The short phrase "the teaching situation" can be cut to "teaching."

The longer phrase "But in analyzing the teaching situation at the
college level" is dangling, because its subject, at least grammatically,
is "upshot," and "upshot" is not "analyzing."

Before we try to amend, though, let's remind ourselves where it
fits. Here again are our opening sentences:

> Every subject presents its own pedagogic problems. Yet whatever the
> topic, teaching always involves the instructor, the student, the mate-
> rial, the method, and the environment, and neglecting any one ele-
> ment will harm the entire process.

After these thoughts, do we really need an introductory phrase or
clause about analyzing college teaching? Hasn't our author been
doing so all along? Therefore let's cut the introductory clause, and
move right into the next thought:

> all too often the student and his interests, attitudes, needs, and prob-
> lems are only given cursory consideration by those involved in struc-
> turing and presenting a course.

Here we encounter more wordiness. For instance, "all too often"
can be trimmed to "too often."

We also observe the singular word "student" and the following
pronoun "his." We're discussing both males and females here, so let's
change "student" to "students" and "his" to "their."

Now we have another four-word sequence: "interests, attitudes,
needs, and problems." Do we need all four? Consider "interests" and

"attitudes." Don't they overlap? Furthermore, "attitudes" has connotations of *arrogance*, so let's cut "attitudes."

How about "needs" and "problems"? Again, these two words seem related. But not every student has "problems," while every student has "needs." Let's strike "problems."

The first half of the sentence now reads:

> Too often the students' interests and needs are only given cursory consideration by . . .

What about "the students'"? Could we dispose of the article and turn "students'" into the simple adjective "student"? The clause now reads:

> Too often student interests and needs are only given cursory consideration by . . .

The word "only" alerts us to its possible misplacement, and, indeed, "only" is in the wrong spot. As the sentence currently reads, "student needs and interests" are "only given." They're not respected, answered, or satisfied. But now move "only" after "given":

> Too often student interests and needs are given only cursory consideration by . . .

As revised, the sentence means that "student interests and needs" are given nothing but "cursory consideration," precisely what our author wishes to say.

How about "those involved in structuring and presenting a course"? Of whom is the author speaking? Professors, we assume. But not all college teachers are professors, and the author may well intend his ideas to extend to classroom instructors beyond the college level. Can we find one word that encompasses all those who teach, whatever their level?

"Faculty" will do. The sentence now stands this way:

> Too often student interests and needs are given only cursory consideration by faculty.

Suddenly we note that the entire construction is in passive voice. Does that work here? To help us decide, let's put the sentence into active voice:

> Too often faculty give student interests and needs only cursory consideration.

Either version is acceptable, but we think that here is one situation where the passive voice is more effective, because using it highlights the students, probably our author's goal.

At last the moment has arrived to put everything we have before us:

> Every subject presents its own pedagogic problems. Yet whatever the topic, teaching always involves the instructor, the student, the material, the method, and the environment, and neglecting any one element will harm the entire process. Too often student interests and needs are given only cursory consideration by faculty.

Better, but the last sentence seems disconnected. We need a transition to indicate that we're considering another side of the crisis. "However" will work. But rather than put it before "Too often," where it will protrude, let's tuck it between later words:

> Too often, however, student interests and needs are given only cursory consideration by faculty.

We have now arrived at the last sentence:

> In my opinion, such factors are crucial to the development of a sound educational experience.

The humble "In my opinion" is superfluous, because the essay contains nothing but the author's judgments. Moreover, such apologies, which include "personally" and "I believe that," rob ensuing ideas of much of their force.

But what about the sentiment as a whole? Is it necessary? The author has already delineated some of what he believes are the components of a good education. Now he reminds us that if those elements are absent, the education will be less effective.

The thought is not needed.

At last we have reached the climactic moment: when we examine what remains of our author's paragraph:

> Every subject presents its own pedagogic problems. Yet whatever the topic, teaching always involves the instructor, the student, the material, the method, and the environment, and neglecting any one element will harm the entire process. Too often, however, student interests and needs are given only cursory consideration by faculty.

Before attempting further rewriting, we'd want to examine this paragraph in the context of the material that surrounds it, and afterward we might want to expand some ideas or tighten others. Thus far, though, we've made substantial progress: pruning excess verbiage, sharpening word choice, and clarifying exactly where we're headed and what the reader should expect.

B. THE SECOND PARAGRAPH

Here's the next paragraph. Again we suggest that you attempt your own revision, then turn to ours.

This second sample appears in the middle of the essay, when our author weighs problems that he has confronted and also asserts the value of what he as a teacher has tried to accomplish:

> As a teacher of mathematics, my belief is that mathematics deserves a place within the liberal arts program, that it is a subject which nonmajors should be exposed to. Mathematics is losing its foothold in the liberal arts program over the past decades with the disappearance of core requirements and the unfavorable attitude developed through a host of negative experiences suffered at the hands of academically incompetent lower school teachers. This is occurring at a time when mathematical techniques are becoming commonplace tools in all areas of human inquiry, and where the failure of students

to be properly exposed to mathematics and the physical sciences results in the unhealthy and unreasoned fear born of ignorance which they direct towards the growing influence of technology. The need to dispel these fears which traditionally envelop the discipline is a central portion of the challenge of teaching mathematics on the college level, to dissolve the confusion which has accompanied the attempts to understand its content, and in effect to save mathematics as an integral part of the liberal arts program and the intellectual toolbox of an individual who wishes to consider himself well-educated or cultured in any sense of these terms.

We see familiar problems, but we'll find new ones as well.

Let's consider the first sentence:

> As a teacher of mathematics, my belief is that mathematics deserves a place within the liberal arts program, that it is a subject which non-majors should be exposed to.

Immediately we note a dangling element: "my belief" is not a "teacher of mathematics." Our initial response, then, is to change "my belief" to "I believe."

Next we see that the sentence concludes with the preposition "to," and prepositions like "to," "in," "on," or "with" in that spot almost always prove awkward. Therefore we change the phrase to read "to which non-majors should be exposed."

Yet even after those minor adjustments, we are struck by more salient errors.

The author has already identified himself as a teacher of mathematics. Does he need to do so again?

We're also dissatisfied with "I believe." By now we understand that this essay proffers the author's own thoughts, so the modest "I believe" may be cut.

Thus we could begin this way:

> Mathematics deserves a place within the liberal arts program.

This solution is possible, but wait. Look at the last sentence of this paragraph and a phrase therein:

> to save mathematics as an integral part of the liberal arts program.

The concept is the same one articulated earlier: mathematics should be restored to its proper place within the liberal arts. Therefore we ask: are both statements necessary? Would one be sufficient? If so, which one? And where should we put it?

To answer these questions, let's go back to the start of the paragraph and reread the second sentence, which begins:

> Mathematics is losing its foothold in the liberal arts program over the past decades.

We'll worry about the sentence structure and wording later. Right now we recognize that the author is about to provide background that explains how and why mathematics has lost its place. What we must decide is whether to state his thesis at the start of the paragraph, then provide the history, or to provide the history first, then follow with the outcome of that series of events.

To resolve this dilemma, we turn to one of our ten basic principles: *place the most dramatic material at the end of sentences.* Here we expand that notion to whole paragraphs and decide to save the thesis statement for the end. Consequently we can eliminate it from the first sentence, and that action means that the entire first sentence disappears, including the second clause, which after our correction reads "that it is a subject to which non-majors should be exposed." This concept will almost certainly be affirmed later: if not in these very words, then by inference.

Now the paragraph begins:

> Mathematics is losing its foothold in the liberal arts program over the past decades with the disappearance of core requirements and the unfavorable attitude developed through a host of negative experiences suffered at the hands of academically incompetent lower school teachers.

The sentence is long, but it packs a lot of information. Hence we want to keep the content, but alter the expression. Our first strategy is to break the entity apart, so here's a possible version of our new first sentence:

> Mathematics is losing its foothold in the liberal arts program over the past decades.

The phrase "over the past decades" belongs at the beginning of the sentence, which would then read:

> Over the past decades, mathematics is losing its foothold in the liberal arts program.

Now, however, we see that the verb is wrong. Because the process in question extends over time, we should be not in present tense, but in present perfect:

> Over the past decades, mathematics has been losing its foothold in the liberal arts program.

"Foothold" is an odd word, but it's striking, so let's leave it. We should, however, cut "program," which refers more to courses at an individual institution than to the overall "liberal arts." In any case, we now have a topic sentence:

> Over the past decade, mathematics has been losing its foothold in the liberal arts.

From this juncture on, all details in the paragraph should either support or amplify that sentence.

To communicate one of the author's explanations for the phenomenon he describes, we create an additional sentence that includes his first idea:

> One reason is the disappearance of core requirements.

Amid so many tortuous expressions, a short, declarative one is welcome. We realize that the curricular movement in question might warrant further discussion, but here is not the place, because our author clearly has other ideas at the fore.

We also remember one of our ten principles: *avoid jargon and bombast*. "Core requirements" may puzzle some readers, but this essay is written for and about teachers, to whom that term will be familiar. Even raising this question, however, suggests another supplementary principle:

Remember your audience

If you are writing for professional historians about the development of the Constitution, you need not identify James Madison. But if you are analyzing the same subject for high school sophomores, you'll have to explain who Madison was. If you write for scholars of Shakespeare, you needn't bother relating that *Richard II* is the story of a weak king whose crown is usurped by political rivals. Sometimes, however, even a learned audience needs help, so if you plan to discuss a new movie or play with which your readers are probably unfamiliar, you'll want to provide details of the plot.

After that brief detour, we return to the author's explanation of why mathematics is losing its foothold:

> A second reason is the unfavorable attitude developed through a host of negative experiences suffered at the hands of academically incompetent lower school teachers.

This reason, pedagogic inadequacy, is clearly our author's primary subject. Thus we want to emphasize that here is where blame lies, and we do so with an insertion:

> A second, more important, reason is the . . .

We've also added a touch of drama. We note, though, the repetition of "reason." Can we find an alternative?

> A second, more important, influence is the unfavorable attitude . . .

Better, but "unfavorable attitude" is unwieldy. Can we find one word to use instead?

> A second, more important, influence is the antagonism . . .

Now we can continue with the sentence:

> developed through a host of . . .

"Developed" has connotations of progress, surely not the author's meaning. Let's change "developed through" to "created by."

> A second, more important, influence is the antagonism created by a host of negative experiences suffered at the hands of . . .

Do we need both "negative experiences" and "suffering"? No. And what about "a host of"? Is it necessary? No.

In addition, the structure of the sentence suggests that the experiences themselves "suffered." Shouldn't we specify that students are the ones enduring pain?

> created by students suffering at the hands of . . .

We like "at the hands of," which implies that bad teaching can wreak damage.

But has the antagonism been created *by* students? Or has it been created *in* students? We think that the author accepts the latter view. Furthermore, as we have already decided, the suffering by students covers a substantial period, so again the present perfect tense fits:

> created in students who have suffered at the hands of . . .

We are using passive voice, but with good reason: we want "students," the subject, to receive the action of the verb "suffered."

Now to the last phrase:

> academically incompetent lower school instructors.

What about "academically"? Does the author believe that these teachers have not mastered their material? He may think that some fall short in this respect, but what matters to him more is that the majority of these instructors, regardless of how many degrees they have earned, are *pedagogically* incompetent. They teach badly. But before we change the adverb "academically," we ask if any modifier is needed at all. Without it, the phrase reads:

> incompetent lower school instructors.

"Incompetent" alone communicates the meaning, so we can cut the adverb.

What about the final phrase: "lower school instructors"? Why not be more specific?

> incompetent elementary, junior high, and high school instructors.

The details make the observation more vivid.

Now let's recapitulate the entire sequence:

> Over the past decades, mathematics has been losing its foothold in the liberal arts. One reason is the disappearance of core requirements. A second, more important, influence is the antagonism created in students who have suffered at the hands of incompetent elementary, junior high, and high school instructors.

We're doing well, so we move to the next sentence:

> This is occurring at a time when mathematical techniques are becoming commonplace tools in all areas of human inquiry, and where the failure of students to be properly exposed to mathematics and the physical sciences results in the unhealthy and unreasoned fear born of ignorance which they direct towards the growing influence of technology.

At once we see a pronoun without an antecedent. What is "This"? We presume that the author means the entire situation, which he believes has serious consequences. One way to solve the problem is to turn "This" into an adjective that modifies a noun we shall choose. To characterize what the author sees as a calamitous trend, the word "crisis" seems appropriate:

> This crisis is occurring at a time when mathematical techniques are becoming commonplace tools in all areas of human inquiry.

This construction isn't bad, but we notice several weaknesses.

First, "at a time when" is wordy. Let's use simply "when."

Second, "commonplace" means "ordinary" or "trite," almost the opposite of what the author intends to say. How about "vital"?

Next, do we need "tools"? Probably not. And as long as we're cutting, do any areas of inquiry *not* involve the "human"? No, so that word can go as well. Finally, is mathematics vital "in all areas of inquiry"? Again, probably not. Scholars of literature rarely summon their skills in trigonometry. Thus let's say "many areas of inquiry."

The revised first part of the sentence now reads:

> This crisis is occurring when mathematical techniques are becoming vital in many areas of inquiry.

The overall construction is running long, so let's end it here, then begin fresh:

> and where the failure of students to be properly exposed to mathematics and the physical sciences results in the unhealthy and unreasoned fear born of ignorance which they direct towards the growing influence of technology.

Here we have only a long clause, not a sentence. Thus we need to cut "and where" and replace it with a transition from the previous thought.

Where do we find one? Earlier in our discussion, we used the word "consequences." Might it not fit here?

> One consequence is the failure . . .

"Consequence" by itself seems mild, for in subsequent lines the author suggests some of the profound effects that have followed the dangerous situation he has described. A well-chosen adjective might help. How about "profound"?

One profound consequence is the failure of students to be properly exposed to mathematics.

But are students the ones who have failed? Or have teachers failed to do right by their students? The author obviously blames the teachers, so we have to shift responsibility, as we do by moving to passive voice:

One profound consequence is that students who have not been properly exposed to mathematics and the physical sciences . . .

Our author has not yet mentioned the physical sciences, but the connection to mathematics seems reasonable, so we'll keep both terms and continue:

results in the unhealthy and unreasoned fear born of ignorance which they direct towards the growing influence of technology.

The way the sentence currently reads, "students" is the subject of the verb "results in." Nor will making the verb plural ("result in") help. "Students" don't "result in." Instead we need a new verb that means "develop." How about "develop"?

develop the unhealthy and unreasoned fear born of ignorance . . .

Do we need the adjectives "unhealthy" and "unreasoned"? What about the phrase "born of ignorance"? Might these qualifiers apply to virtually all apprehensions? Why not just use "a fear"?

develop a fear which they direct toward the growing . . .

We sense wordiness again. How about striking "which they direct toward" and replacing it with a simple "of"?

fear of the growing influence of technology.

We're finished with this sentence, so let's see how the last two constructions read:

This crisis is occurring when mathematical techniques are becoming vital in many areas of inquiry. One profound consequence is that students who have not been properly exposed to mathematics and the physical sciences develop a fear of the growing influence of technology.

We confess that although we originally thought the sentence too long, and therefore divided it, now the pair seems choppy. Thus we restore "and" between them, so that the corrected version reads:

> This crisis is occurring when mathematical techniques are becoming vital in many areas of inquiry, and one profound consequence is that students who have not been properly exposed to mathematics and the physical sciences develop a fear of the growing influence of technology.

The revision is much smoother.

At last we reach the finale of the paragraph:

> The need to dispel these fears which traditionally envelop the discipline is a central portion of the challenge of teaching mathematics on the college level, to dissolve the confusion which has accompanied the attempts to understand its content, and in effect to save mathematics as an integral part of the liberal arts program and the intellectual toolbox of an individual who wishes to consider himself well-educated or cultured in any sense of these terms.

An awkward statement, to say the least. But if we slice through some modifiers, we find the core meaning:

> The need to dispel these fears . . . is a central portion of the challenge . . .

This structure is backwards. We understand that the author wishes to link the previous sentence to this one, so he has repeated "fears," but a single transition word will suffice: "Therefore." It allows us to reverse the clauses and make the sentence more energetic:

> Therefore a central portion of the challenge of teaching mathematics on the college level is the need to dispel these fears which traditionally envelop the discipline.

But we can cut still further.

First, the phrase "a central portion of the challenge" can be reduced to "one challenge."

We can also eliminate some of "the need to dispel these fears" and leave "to dispel these fears."

Finally, in the previous sentence the author mentioned "one fear." Here he writes about "fears." Let's keep the word singular, and do the same with the adjective "these." Now we have:

> Therefore one challenge of teaching mathematics on the college level is to dispel this fear . . .

What about the modifying phrase that follows: "to dissolve the confusion which has accompanied the attempts to understand its content"? It seems both wordy and repetitive, so we omit it.

The following clause, however, is crucial:

> and in effect to save mathematics as an integral part of the liberal arts program . . .

Here is the climax of the paragraph, so we'll keep the ideas intact. We shall, however, cut "in effect," which adds little. We'll also change "save" to "restore," a word that has connotations of *value* and also suggests that mathematics was once regarded as intrinsic to the liberal arts.

Note that the word "mathematics" has recurred too often, so this time we'll use "the subject."

Next, the phrase "as an integral part of" doesn't flow, so let's instead write "to its place in."

Our last move will be to cut the repetitive "to" before "save" and again cut "program," which we excised from the first sentence.

The first part of this sentence now reads:

> Therefore one challenge of teaching mathematics on the college level is to dispel this fear and restore the subject to its place in the liberal arts.

And now to the concluding clause:

and the intellectual toolbox of any individual who wishes to consider himself well-educated or cultured in any sense of these terms.

The image "intellectual toolbox" is jarring, but it reflects the author's own voice, so let's keep it. We can try other adjustments, though.

"Intellectual toolbox" has comic overtones, but the conjunction "and" after "liberal arts" suggests that "liberal arts" and "intellectual toolbox" deserve equal stature. If, however, we change "and" to "as well as," we reduce the significance of "intellectual toolbox."

The usage "wishes to" before "consider" implies *longing* and therefore weakens the verb, so let's cut "wishes to." Moreover, to keep the sentence gender-neutral, let's also make "individual" plural and change "himself" to "themselves."

As for the last phrase, "cultured in any sense of these terms," it adds nothing, so we'll dispense with it.

Here, then, is the revised last sentence:

> Therefore one challenge of teaching mathematics on the college level is to dispel this fear and restore the subject to its place in the liberal arts as well as the intellectual toolbox of any individuals who consider themselves well-educated.

The noun "place" seems bland. To enrich it, let's add a spirited modifier: "honored."

Now here's the entire paragraph:

> Over the past decades, mathematics has been losing its foothold in the liberal arts. One reason is the disappearance of core requirements. A second, more important, influence is the antagonism created in students who have suffered at the hands of incompetent elementary, junior high, and high school instructors. This crisis is occurring when mathematical techniques are becoming vital in many areas of inquiry, and one profound consequence is that students who have not been properly exposed to mathematics and the physical sciences develop a fear of the growing influence of technology. Therefore one challenge of teaching mathematics on the college level is to dispel this fear and restore the subject to its honored place in the liberal arts as well as

the intellectual toolbox of any individuals who consider themselves well-educated.

The passage starts quietly and grows increasingly urgent. We're finished with it.

C. THE THIRD PARAGRAPH

Here is our third paragraph, which appears at the conclusion of the essay. Because the author is summing up, we expect to find repetition of words, phrases, and ideas, and we certainly do, but we also realize that he intends to leave us with a measure of hope and even inspiration. Our job is to help him.

> Needless to say, this aura of fear which surrounds the study of mathematics has resulted both in a reverence and respect for those who have successfully mastered its intricate and elusive concepts. The homage paid the mathematicians and the mathematics major has served to kindle an attitude within the mathematics establishment which tends to treat the mathematically competent as the intellectual superiors of those who have proven themselves in other disciplines. Such academic chauvinism (not unique to mathematicians) has the damaging effect of insulating the mathematical community. This acts to the detriment of the educational process, for it serves to alienate the uninitiated, hence perpetuating the attitudes of awe, hostility, fear, etc. commonly directed toward the discipline, thus impeding any efforts between those who know and those who do not to generate sound communication. The teacher of mathematics, if he wishes to preserve the subject as a vital component of the liberal arts program, must be prepared to extend himself to generate the kind of enthusiasm for the discipline which can only be attained through a structured and stimulating approach to its material, presented in a setting which respects the integrity of the subject while recognizing the needs, attitudes, and dignity of the student.

On we go.

The opening phrase "Needless to say" invites immediate cutting. If something need not be said, why say it? On occasion you'll want to suggest that readers might be familiar with a thought, but you're not sure. In that case, preface "needless to say" with "perhaps," a subtle way to communicate your predicament. At this point, however, our author knows that his readers have been immersed in the concepts to follow, so the cautionary modifier should be eliminated.

Here, then, is the new opening of the conclusion:

This aura of fear which surrounds the study of mathematics . . .

Again our author has reverted to wordiness. "This aura of fear" may be reduced to "This fear." We have, however, used "fear" so often that we should use a synonym. "Anxiety" seems appropriate. It denotes "dread," but also "anticipation," and as such captures the spirit of the emotion.

This substitution leads us to one more supplementary principle:

Use a variety of words

While recurring vocabulary often induces monotony, a fresh selection of words usually piques interest. You may wonder where we find our alternative word choices, and one answer is a thesaurus or synonym book that we urge you to keep at the ready. We're not encouraging you to ravage this volume, then show off polysyllabic curiosities. But if you believe that your piece has begun to plod because of repetitious words or phrases, take time to search for new ones.

By the way, one way to discover damaging repetition is to recite your piece out loud. Many errors that escape notice when you read silently become obvious when you speak and thereby hear your writing.

Back to the essay and the sentence currently under examination:

This aura of fear which surrounds the study of mathematics . . .

What about the rest of the phrase: "which surrounds the study of mathematics"? This construction, too, is verbose. True, anxiety does "surround" mathematics, but the problem is more direct. We also know that mathematics is a "study." Why not say simply "about mathematics"? The revised opening now reads:

> This anxiety about mathematics . . .

We're ready to move ahead.

> has resulted both in a reverence and respect for those who have successfully mastered its intricate and elusive concepts.

Here we need a good deal of work.

First, "both" is misplaced. As it currently sits, "both" requires that we include a parallel word after "in." For instance, this sentence might correctly read "both *in and out* of the classroom." If, however, "both" comes *after* "in," a proper sentence might be "in both the classroom and the library." Our author wants "both" to encompass two words: "reverence" and "respect." Thus he should have written "has resulted in both a reverence and respect for those . . ."

Let's return to the sentence:

> has resulted in both a reverence and respect for those who have successfully mastered its intricate and elusive concepts.

Despite our adjustment with "in" and "both," the writing remains weak. "Resulted in" uses two words where one might suffice, but we've used "caused" a lot. The same with "created." How about "engendered"?

> has engendered both a reverence and respect for those who have successfully mastered its intricate and elusive concepts.

Aren't "reverence" and "respect" close in meaning? Yes, so one should servee. We choose "reverence," which not only is more interesting but also implies religious fervor, a sentiment in line with the author's thesis.

Next, the author writes "successfully mastered." Can anyone *unsuccessfully* master something? No, so "master" alone would be fine.

But can we find a word for those who "have mastered" a subject? How about the obvious "masters"?

Finally, we have "intricate and elusive," another pair of words that are close in meaning. They're different enough, however, that cutting one might blunt the author's point. Can we find a single word that incorporates both? We think "abstruse" does the job.

Here, at last, is the revised first sentence:

> This anxiety about mathematics has engendered a reverence for masters of its abstruse concepts.

Now to the next:

> The homage paid the mathematician and the mathematics major has served to kindle an attitude within the mathematics establishment that tends to treat the mathematically competent as the intellectual superiors of those who have proven themselves in other disciplines.

"Homage" is a strong word, so let's keep it. But do we need both "the mathematician" and "the mathematics major"? No, so let's omit "the mathematics major," which falls under the scope of "the mathematician." Still, the concept of *deference* has already been invoked to characterize what is given to its "masters." Therefore let's change "the homage" to "such homage," so that we no longer need to amplify "homage" by explaining to whom it is being "paid." Now "the mathematician" can disappear, too, and we are left with:

> Such homage has served to kindle . . .

How about "served to kindle"? Here's an opportunity to cut "served to" and leave "kindle," but in past tense: "kindled."

At this juncture we read "an attitude within the mathematics establishment that . . ." This construction works, but we think it will be improved if we place the modifying phrase "within the mathematics establishment" directly after "kindled." Doing so will leave the pronoun "that" adjacent to its antecedent, "attitude."

> Such homage has kindled within the mathematics establishment an attitude that tends to treat . . .

Yet even as we write this phrase, we recognize that the word "mathematics" has recurred too often. Instead let's use "the subject's establishment." This opening of the sentence now reads:

> Such homage has kindled within the subject's establishment an attitude that tends to treat . . .

When we read "tends to treat," our reaction is swift: cut "tends to" and leave "treat," but with an *s* on the end.

The next few words are solid: "the mathematically competent as the intellectual superiors." No changes needed.

The last phrase of the sentence is "of those who have proven themselves in other disciplines." Can we find something more concise? Those who have proven themselves in any discipline are called "scholars." How about "other scholars"?

With these adjustments completed, the second sentence reads:

> Such homage has kindled within the subject's establishment an attitude that treats the mathematically competent as the intellectual superiors of other scholars.

Suddenly, however, we see a new error. Does the "attitude" really "treat" the "mathematically competent"? No, "the establishment" in fact "treats." Thus so we can eliminate "an attitude that," we need to strike "kindled within" and insert a verb that describes how this homage has affected "the establishment." We consider "inspired," but that word has positive connotations. Eventually we come upon "misled," which denotes *fallen into error*, exactly the idea we want. Here's the revision:

> Such homage has misled the subject's establishment to treat the mathematically competent as the intellectual superiors of other scholars.

All that's missing is a link between the effect this sentence describes and the one clarified in the previous sentence. A single word will provide that connection: "also" inserted before "misled." Now the two sentences read:

This anxiety about mathematics has engendered a reverence for masters of its abstruse concepts. Such homage has also misled the subject's establishment to treat the mathematically competent as the intellectual superiors of other scholars.

We move on:

Such academic chauvinism (not unique to mathematicians) has the damaging effect of insulating the mathematical community.

The first three words, "Such academic chauvinism," are powerful, so we'll keep them, along with the gentle reminder that follows in parentheses. But even that phrase can be improved. Instead of "not unique," let's write "hardly unique," which has a touch of elegance.

The author also writes that "academic chauvinism" is not "unique to mathematicians." We've noted several times that variations of "mathematicians" recur throughout both this paragraph and the essay. Why not eliminate the word here and simultaneously make the observation more general?

Such academic chauvinism (hardly unique to any discipline) has the damaging effect of insulating the mathematical community.

The next combination of words, however, is verbose. Do we need "the damaging effect" as well as "insulating"? The implication of "insulation" is itself negative. Then let's say simply "insulates the mathematical community." The sentence now reads:

Such academic chauvinism (hardly unique to any discipline) insulates the mathematical community.

This tactic takes us directly to the next thought:

This acts to the detriment of the educational process, for it serves to alienate the uninitiated, hence perpetuating the attitudes of awe, hostility, fear, etc. commonly directed toward the discipline, thus impeding any efforts between those who know and those who do not to generate sound communication.

The opening pronoun "this" lacks an antecedent, but before we try to provide one, we notice the word "detriment," which, like "insulates," implies *damage*. Can we remove "detriment"? As we weigh how to do so, we realize the phrase "the educational process" is probably superfluous as well, because the entire essay is about education. Finally, "serves to alienate" can be trimmed to "alienate."

What we need, then, is a direct bridge from "insulates the mathematical community" in the previous sentence to "alienate the uninitiated" in this one, and after a moment's cogitation, we find it:

> and alienates the uninitiated . . .

The antithesis between "insulates the mathematical community" and "alienates the uninitiated" is effective. The first denotes *turning inward* while the second suggests *turning away*. The construction is also another example of parallel structure:

> Such academic chauvinism (hardly unique to any discipline) insulates the mathematical community and alienates the uninitiated.

Now we can continue with the sentence:

> hence perpetuating the attitudes of awe, hostility, and fear, etc. . . .

We see that "attitudes of" may be cut, leaving "awe, hostility, and fear, etc." Do we need all three? "Awe" suggests being overwhelmed, by either wonder or terror, so the one word alone suffices.

The use of a single noun also eliminates the need for "etc.," which does not belong here anyway. It should be used only when the sequence is predictable: e.g., "1, 2, 3, etc." When the reader cannot be certain what will follow, as in "London, Paris, Cairo, etc." the device should be avoided.

Now the phrase reads:

> hence perpetuating the awe commonly directed toward the discipline . . .

Earlier in the sentence we used "discipline," so here let's substitute "field." This construction is followed by:

thus impeding any efforts . . .

The conjunction "thus" implies that "impeding" is a result of "perpetuating." But "impeding" is a corollary of "perpetuating," and equally significant. Therefore we prefer "and" before "impeding."

After that minor change, the final section reads:

> hence perpetuating the awe commonly directed toward the field and impeding any efforts between those who know and those who do not to generate sound communication.

Our first instinct is to slip "to generate sound communication" right after "efforts," the word that the phrase modifies:

> and impeding any efforts to generate sound communication between those who know and those who do not.

Yet we still have a verbose locution. What we can do instead is strike "any efforts to generate" ("any" was always unnecessary) and leave "sound communication." After realizing that "sound communication" is redundant, we omit "sound":

> and impeding communication between those who know and those who do not.

We pause to consider the use of "between." That word applies when a relationship or conversation takes place between two individuals. When three or more are involved, "among" is correct. Here, however, two groups of people are mentioned, so "between" fits. The same principle applies to "each other," which refers to two entities, and "one another," which refers to three or more.

Now back to the sentence. The words are short, but we find an excess of them. What's our alternative? Well, who are the ones who "know"? Those who work in the discipline of mathematics. Who doesn't "know"? Those who work in other disciplines. What do we call communication between those in different disciplines? "Interdisciplinary communication." It may smack of jargon, but we think readers will recognize it. Therefore our final phrase now reads:

and impeding interdisciplinary communication.

Now how does the entire sentence sound?

> Such academic chauvinism (hardly unique to any discipline) insulates the mathematical community and alienates the uninitiated, hence perpetuating the awe commonly directed toward the field and impeding interdisciplinary communication.

At last we're prepared to examine what we've done:

> This anxiety about mathematics has engendered a reverence for masters of its abstruse concepts. Such homage has also misled the subject's establishment to treat the mathematically competent as the intellectual superiors of other scholars. Such academic chauvinism (hardly unique to any discipline) insulates the mathematical community and alienates the uninitiated, hence perpetuating the awe commonly directed toward the field and impeding interdisciplinary communication.

The passage is improved, but one construction continues to bother us: "perpetuating the awe commonly directed toward the field." The concept has been repeated so often that we think it has become unnecessary. Thus even though we admire our choice of "awe," we cut the entire phrase. Then we change the earlier "discipline" to "field," a tactic that allows us to avoid even a hint of repetition (created by "discipline" and "interdisciplinary"):

> This anxiety about mathematics has engendered a reverence for masters of its abstruse concepts. Such homage has also misled the subject's establishment to treat the mathematically competent as the intellectual superiors of other scholars. Such academic chauvinism (hardly unique to any field) insulates the mathematical community and alienates the uninitiated, hence impeding interdisciplinary communication.

We're ready to proceed:

> The teacher of mathematics, if he wishes to preserve the subject as a vital component of the liberal arts program, must be prepared to

extend himself to generate the kind of enthusiasm for the discipline which can be only attained through a structured and stimulating approach to its material, presented in a setting which respects the integrity of the subject while recognizing the needs, attitudes, and dignity of the student.

In reading this final sentence, we notice that the first half of the paragraph, the part we've edited, focuses on problems. But this second half, which we've yet to tackle, is concerned more with solutions. It also offers inspiration for the goals to be achieved. Therefore we take an unexpected step: to turn this last sentence into a new paragraph, the final one of the essay.

To clarify that we're concluding, let's begin with a word that signals our intention: "thus." Now let's look at the rest of the sentence.

"The teacher of mathematics" needs to be made plural, and as we insert that change, we convert "he" in the following subordinate clause to "they":

Thus teachers of mathematics, if they wish to preserve the subject as a vital component of the liberal arts program . . .

To clarify our meaning, though, and to be more dramatic, we should put the subordinate clause first:

Thus if they wish to preserve the subject as a vital component of the liberal arts program, teachers of mathematics . . .

Now, however, the first "they" has no antecedent. Therefore we switch "they" in the subordinate clause with "teachers of mathematics" in the main clause:

Thus if teachers of mathematics wish to preserve the subject as a vital component of the liberal arts program, they . . .

As we did earlier, we cut "program" after "liberal arts." Now, however, the pronoun "they" refers to "arts." To eliminate this problem, we want "teachers of mathematics" to lead directly to the verb that follows. Let's therefore cut "if," and make "teachers of mathematics" the subject of the main clause, not the dependent one.

> Thus teachers of mathematics wish to preserve the subject as a vital component . . .

Remember, though, we're not referring to all teachers of mathematics, only those who "wish to preserve the subject." Therefore we need to qualify those instructors, so let's add "who" after "mathematics." This revision leaves us with:

> Thus teachers of mathematics who wish to preserve the subject as a vital component of the liberal arts . . .

> Now we continue, maintaining the plural subject and verb:

> must be prepared to extend themselves to generate the kind of enthusiasm for the discipline which can be only attained through a structured and stimulating approach to its material.

Once more we sense verbosity, so let's look at the first several words: "must be prepared to extend themselves to generate." What is the core meaning here? That teachers must generate enthusiasm. Then let's use precisely those words:

> Thus teachers of mathematics who wish to preserve the subject as a vital component of the liberal arts must generate enthusiasm for the discipline . . .

We know that the object of that enthusiasm is "mathematics," so let's cut "for the discipline," simultaneously avoiding another repetition of the root "discipline." What follows?

> which can be only attained through a structured and stimulating approach to its material . . .

Because we have eliminated so many words, we must make the clause restrictive (the information therein is essential). Therefore "which" should be changed to "that."

We also question the placement of "only." Does our author mean that the "enthusiasm" he describes can "be only attained"? That it cannot be admired or developed? No, he means that such enthusiasm can be "attained only" if certain conditions are met "through a structured and stimulating approach." Finally, "to its material" is obvious and therefore superfluous.

Now the sentence reads:

> Thus teachers of mathematics who wish to preserve the subject as a vital component of the liberal arts must generate enthusiasm that can be attained only through a structured and stimulating approach.

We like the alliterative "st" sounds of "structured and stimulating." More important, because we're at the end of the essay, shorter, strong sentences will be more powerful, so let's end this one here.

We now move to the last clause. At the moment it reads:

> presented in a setting which respects the integrity of the subject while recognizing the needs, attitudes, and dignity of the student.

We want this sentiment to become the concluding sentence, so before we do anything else, we need to supply a subject and a verb for "presented. "This" will do, because its clear antecedent is "approach." The verb "must be" will also work, although once again, because the clause is restrictive, we'll change "which" to "that":

> This must be presented in a setting that respects the integrity of the subject while recognizing . . .

The participle phrase "while recognizing" weakens the impact of the idea, so for emphasis let's maintain parallel verbs:

> respects the integrity of the subject and recognizes the needs, attitudes, and dignity of the student.

The alliterative *r* sounds of "respects" and "recognizes" also earn our approval, but to make them resound even more effectively, let's insert "both" before "respects":

> This must be presented in a setting that both respects the integrity of the subject and recognizes the needs, attitudes, and dignity of the student.

With these changes incorporated, the final paragraph reads:

Thus teachers of mathematics who wish to preserve the subject as a vital component of the liberal arts must generate enthusiasm that can be attained only through a structured and stimulating approach. This must be presented in a setting that respects the integrity of the subject and recognizes the needs, attitudes, and dignity of the student.

We think all three words in the sequence "needs, attitude, and dignity" contribute something, so we'll leave them.

Here, then, are the final two paragraphs of the essay:

This anxiety about mathematics has engendered a reverence for masters of its abstruse concepts. Such homage has also misled the subject's establishment to treat the mathematically competent as the intellectual superiors of other scholars. Such academic chauvinism (hardly unique to any field) insulates that community and alienates the uninitiated, hence impeding interdisciplinary communication.

Thus teachers of mathematics who wish to preserve the subject as a vital component of the liberal arts must generate enthusiasm that can be attained only through a structured and stimulating approach. This must be presented in a setting that respects the integrity of the subject and recognizes the needs, attitudes, and dignity of the student.

We have at last finished.

CONCLUSION

What have we accomplished?

First we considered ten basic editing strategies; then during our rewriting efforts added three more. In the meantime, we applied all of them to improving three particularly challenging passages.

We would never claim, however, that our methods are the only ones that work. The paragraphs that we have considered could have been refined in other acceptable ways, for just as great actors can interpret a role from different perspectives and with different techniques, so writers can succeed with their own styles.

Incidentally, you may wonder why we have not provided additional passages for you to edit on your own. The answer is simple: now that you've had all this practice, you'll be eager to concentrate on your own work.

We also want to emphasize that the editing process is rarely straightforward. You no doubt noticed that during our exertions, we constantly reread and reconsidered our choices. Even when we assumed that we had finished a section, we found more to change.

This realization brings us to our final point. The process of writing and rewriting is unending. Careful writers can tinker forever, so that anyone who vows to submit only a perfect manuscript is doomed to despair. Indeed, almost all of us can point to alterations we would make in articles or books that we published years earlier.

You're in a similar position. You compose a draft, then reread and revise, perhaps on the basis of the strategies suggested here. That process could extend forever, but eventually you'll want to submit your work. You understand that you won't ever be totally satisfied, but at least you can trust that whatever editing you've completed will have improved your product.

We certainly hope so.

EPILOGUE

Here, as promised, are two samples of our own work. Each is autobiographical and describes a seminal experience from our education. As you will see, however, they contrast notably in tone and theme.

When you read these pieces, you may discover that we've violated some of our own rules. If so, we like to think that the results vindicate us.

TURNING POINT

Steven M. Cahn

In 1963, having just received my bachelor's degree from Columbia College, I enrolled as a graduate student in Columbia University's Department of Philosophy. I was unsure, however, that I was taking the right step, and wondered whether I ought instead to have been attending law school, embarking on a doctoral program in American history, or studying piano at a conservatory.

As I looked through the semester's offerings, I came upon a course titled "Philosophical Analysis." I had no idea what it was about and was unfamiliar with the instructor, Richard Taylor, who had recently come to Columbia from Brown, but, taking a chance, I enrolled.

The next afternoon I entered the department's luxurious seminar room, sat in one of the plush chairs, and with about thirty other students awaited the appearance of our professor. When he arrived, he began by telling us that this course would be different from others we might have taken. We would not study the writings of famous philosophers of the past or pore over learned commentaries about them. Rather, we would *do* philosophy. We would not read about philosophers; we would ourselves *be* philosophers. Having spent many undergraduate hours struggling with knotty works written centuries before, I welcomed whatever he had in mind.

He informed us that the reading for the course would consist of only a few articles, and that we would be writing three papers in which we ourselves tried to solve the very issues discussed in those articles. I found this plan hard to believe. Bertrand Russell or John Dewey might solve a philosophical problem, but how could I? After all, I was taking my first graduate course, and I had mastered few of the classics. How could I solve a philosophical problem? And who would be interested in reading my views?

Professor Taylor next told us that the first article we were to discuss had not yet appeared in print. This announcement added to my surprise, because I had never read a professional article prior to publication. He proceeded to distribute mimeographed pages by a scholar unknown to me. Our assignment, we were told, was to analyze this essay and decide whether its main contention was correct.

Professor Taylor then approached the chalkboard, wrote several statements, and asked whether the last statement followed from the previous ones.

A student raised his hand and launched into a long speech full of technical terms and references to the works of several medieval thinkers. As Professor Taylor listened intently, his face expressed first hope, then disappointment. "I'm afraid I don't understand much of what you said," he replied. "I didn't ask anything about any medieval philosophers. I asked only if the last statement is implied by the previous ones. What do you think?" The student shrugged and looked frustrated.

Another student confidently raised her hand and inquired whether the issue had not been handled adequately in an article that had appeared many years before in a leading philosophical journal. Professor Taylor responded, "I really don't know. I haven't read that article. But perhaps you could tell us: is the last sentence I have written on the blackboard implied by the previous ones?" The student replied that she couldn't remember. "But," he continued, "there's nothing to remember. The statements are on the board. Does the last follow from the others, or doesn't it?" She offered no reply.

Never in my study of philosophy had I witnessed such an approach. I was unfamiliar with the medieval thinkers to whom the first student had referred, and I knew nothing of the article to which the second student had alluded. The answer to the professor's question, however, was not to be found in a dog-eared tome or a dusty journal. We were being asked to think, to philosophize.

Suddenly I understood what Professor Taylor had meant when he said we would try to solve philosophical problems, and at that moment I experienced a remarkable liberation. I raised my hand and presented my opinion, something I had been reluctant to do in other classes, for fear my ignorance of philosophical literature would be apparent to all. Professor Taylor indicated that my comment was intriguing, but inquired how I would deal with a certain objection. I was unsure and sat silently, pondering. By the time an answer came to me, the class was over.

I decided to visit him and pursue my point. Other professors were usually available for conferences with students only three or four hours a week. Professor Taylor met with his students three or four *afternoons* a week—for several hours each afternoon. I was accustomed to waiting on line to see a popular teacher, but Professor Taylor placed a sheet on his office door so students could sign up in advance for fifteen- or thirty-minute appointments.

The next day I ventured in and began presenting my ideas. Before long, though, he interrupted: "Write a paper for me." I had not intended to write down my views, believing that I needed only to communicate them orally, but he clearly indicated that putting ideas into writing was indispensable to precise thinking.

I returned home, worked harder than I could remember, and the following week brought him a paper. He told me he would read it and get back to me. Several days later, eager to learn his reaction, I knocked on his door before the announced office hours and timidly inquired whether he had read my essay. He replied that he was busy writing and could not speak with me, but would return the paper. He passed it through the half-open door and said he would see me later. On the front page was his comment, the substance of which was that after further work, the paper ought to be published, then serve as a section of my dissertation.

I was stunned. Here I was in the first month of graduate study, and told not only that I had written something worth publishing, but that I had already, in essence, completed part of my dissertation.

For the next two years I devoted myself to justifying his confidence. I attended every class he taught and wrote paper after paper. I signed up for conferences several times a week and often waited near his office to take advantage of free time created by the cancellation of a scheduled appointment. He never begrudged me a moment but continued urging me to write more and come in to discuss what I had written. The hours we spent together became the focus of my life.

I no longer doubted my choice of career and through his patience and efforts I became a philosopher. Incidentally, his reaction to that first paper proved prophetic, because three years after writing it, I received my Ph.D., and my dissertation included the already published material from that initial piece.

Richard Taylor died in 2003, but whenever I meet with graduate students to offer them advice, I think of him. I remember with deep gratitude his invaluable guidance that enabled me to overcome my misgivings and find my way through the world of academia. He provided my inspiration, and for that gift I shall always be grateful.

Earlier versions of this material appeared in my book *From Student to Scholar: A Candid Guide to Becoming a Professor* (New York: Columbia University Press, 2008), 75–78; and in my book *Saints and Scamps: Ethics in Academia*, 25th Anniversary Edition (Lanham, MD: Rowman & Littlefield, 2011), 92–95. The essay is reprinted with permission of Rowman & Littlefield Publishers.

THE UNIVERSE AND DR. CAHN

Victor L. Cahn

When I was fourteen and a sophomore in high school, I one day found myself in Brentano's bookstore in New York City, holding a work titled *The Universe and Dr. Einstein* by Lincoln Barnett. The volume was slim, so I was immediately attracted by it, as I am by all slim volumes. I sense a crystalline perfection in a book that says all in a few pages. Slim volumes have a magic about them, a purity that tingles. Fat volumes may have heft and majesty, but rarely do they tingle.

The title as well appealed to me. True, my knowledge of physics was nil, but Einstein's name was alluring, and the cover blurb proclaimed that this book contained the essence of his theory of relativity, as well as an array of other abstruse matters. I sensed power at my fingertips. If by chance I could digest these words, if I could grasp their pith, I would have much of twentieth-century science at my command. I would have Einstein and his grand vision in my intellectual hip pocket. And I could reveal him at choice moments, to leave both students and teachers agape with wonder.

The purchase was completed, and I went home a-tingling. That evening, with a little trepidation, I began to read. I should not be considered boastful to report that over the next few nights I did complete the work, and even understood certain parts, now, of course, long forgotten. But I believe that for a fleeting moment I actually had some sense of what relativity was all about. The book was that good.

At the time, however, I was impressed with myself. So impressed, in fact, that I imagined I had found my calling. My world was physics. Forget those struggles through general science and biology. Forget the travails of plane geometry. I was meant for bigger things.

Relativity. The world. The Universe! I envisioned the grand scheme, the great continuum of existence. When I glanced at my assignments in French and history, I shook my head. The piddling academic grind was no longer for me. My realm was the heavens.

Not long after this epiphany, I came across a summer school catalogue from Phillips Academy in Andover, Massachusetts. Glancing through, I reached the science offerings and a course called "Basic Concepts of Physics."

Physics. My world. My thing.

Yet would the challenge be sufficient? "Basic Concepts" had a juvenile tone, and I was not interested in mere basics, for I was already involved in relativity. But I relented, for surely I could pick up a few pointers even in this elementary course. Admittedly, I had never studied physics, except on my own, so perhaps I could use a brush-up. I reasoned further that so short a course would not intrude on my own projects. In other words, the six weeks would be well spent, if a mite boring.

I applied to the program (then all-male), was naturally accepted, and sat back in anticipation. Would I major in physics in college? That was the best place to start, where facilities and professors waited at the ready. Everyone started there. I would, too.

Then on to graduate school, for a master's degree and a doctorate. Yet I would not allow myself to be weighed down by academic rigmarole. I would also use the time to develop a network of colleagues, to learn professional ins and outs. And I would have opportunities, for my work would not demand twenty-four hours a day. I would have to take a break. Hobbies, for instance. Maybe I'd learn to plant a garden, another way to be at one with nature. That seemed a particularly scientific thing to do, something physical, even relative. Perhaps I could sow carrots and string beans. Then when reporters came to interview me, I would offer them a salad grown right in my own backyard.

How humble I would be. How charming for a great mind to occupy itself with the modest aspects of life.

With my doctorate I would teach, perhaps at Harvard, perhaps at somewhere rural. I relished picturesque settings, so Cal Tech was a possibility. I knew I was jumping the gun, for I'd have to consider carefully specific offers, but options would be myriad.

I would profit as well by continuing to study the violin. Einstein had created a healthy image for himself, although I did not want to be regarded as a crass imitator. But music and physics seemed to complement each other so neatly: the cold scientific domain of physics and the warm emotionalism of music. Not to mention my garden (with the home-grown salads). The press would eat it up. Ha-ha.

Eventually my success would be renowned worldwide, and my workplace would become a shrine. Like Edison's, it would be known as the home of "The Wizard of . . . Someplace Rural." How else would they honor me? A nickname was a start, but even minor figures had nicknames. No doubt a university laboratory would be named after me, perhaps a building or two on the campus where I'd work and where the library would store my papers. But I didn't intend to be strictly a local celebrity. No, I'd also be the recipient of a list of awards presented by a grateful nation and world. Certainly a Nobel Prize was in the offing. I had to receive my Nobel Prize. Every famous physicist I knew had one.

Then I conceived a surer sign of immortality. Someone would name a unit of measurement after me: a "cahn."

A cahn. What a lovely sound. Four watts, three volts, two amps, and a cahn.

What would a cahn measure? Something to do with physics, of course. Something very relative, perhaps with atoms.

The distance across the span of a proton.

A cahn.

I envisioned physics instructors of the future demanding of their students: "I'd like that answer in cahns, please. Answers strictly in cahns."

Perhaps my colleagues in the lab would also bestow a personal gift. When they created a new element, they would name it after me: "cahnium." That tribute would especially please me, because it would come from my friends, the men and women with whom I had worked most closely.

Finally I'd receive the greatest accolade of all. I might not live to see it, but little matter. Physics would henceforth be divided into two eras: B.C. and A.C. Before Cahn and After.

I was satisfied. The world would long remember me, as well it should.

At last school registration day arrived. Did I exude confidence when I entered the administration building to receive my schedule and dormitory key? I reflected that one day biographers would retrace these very steps.

Early that evening I wandered about the campus, until I came to Evans Hall, the science building. I had heard that it was impressive, and indeed it was. Of course, it had been completed only a year or two before.

They had known I was coming.

To my surprise, a door was open, and I toured the hallways, guided by the soft glow of twilight. The labs were attractive and spotless, and all the equipment I would need for my work was available. Here was a proper place for the great adventure to begin. Nothing would hold me back.

That night in the dormitory, as I became acquainted with other residents, I was properly diffident. When asked which course I had elected, I replied simply, "Physics." Just like that. No fanfare, no grandiose statements. Antagonizing my listeners would do no good. Humble, ever humble, was my byword. Let them discover my presence later, then revel in the brilliance. Quality need not advertise.

Before classes began, my chief responsibility was to obtain textbooks. For physics I was required to buy *College Physics* and a slide rule. *College Physics* sounded satisfactory, for at least I would not have to endure some petty high school course. The slide rule would help, of course, although I had never handled one before. (During the early 1960s, the time of this tale, calculators and computers were not available.) But after a couple of minutes' attention I would have no difficulty. After all, it was an important tool. I couldn't spend my scientific life drowning in long division. Or did people in labs specialize in that sort of work? I would investigate.

At last Monday morning arrived. The dawn broke, and with it a bright ray of sunshine glittered upon me.

The moment was here.

I dressed calmly. My image would suffer if I rushed headlong, the characteristically befogged scientist. Instead, an easy manner would do much more towards cultivating the proper demeanor. Brilliance and sloppiness were not necessarily intertwined, and a measure of style was perfectly compatible with genius. Even in my garden I would not look grubby. I would wear slacks and a sports shirt so that no bony knees would protrude. A tie might be a bit much.

With dignity I made my way across campus. How would my biographer describe the moment? "Across the green plushness he strode, onward to immortality." A bit purplish, but a writer was entitled to license. In the movie, organ music would swell in the background. A choir? No, too early in the plot. That would come later. With the awarding of the Medal of Freedom? Much better.

At last I reached Evans Hall, where my career would begin. I opened the door, and let it close gently behind me. My footsteps echoed down the corridor. Perhaps in the movie the camera would pan upward for a cathedral effect, to hint that a divine order permeates the universe. Subtle, but keener critics would grasp it.

After a left turn, I opened a door that revealed the custodial closet. But with scarcely a breath, I reversed myself, took another hallway, and eventually came upon the classroom: Number 12. I paused outside. I felt no need to hurry. I checked my textbook, my slide rule, and the spiral notebook I had purchased. One day it would probably be encased in a library display.

All was in order. I entered.

Twelve boys sat silently at their desks. No one looked at me. With what I fear was a hint of arrogance, I strutted to my seat. Perhaps "strutted" is too strong. "Swaggered"? No. I was not as pompous as that, either. "Sauntered"? No, not even that. My biographer would have it right. I "strode." I took my seat at the back. I wanted perspective on events. Scientific detachment.

I looked at the students. Here I might have said "the other students." Yet clearly I was not one of them. I was a world unto myself, following my own program, my own "schedule with destiny," as my biographer would note.

As I perused them, a few chatted quietly. Did they know? Did they intuit my presence? Did they sense the grandeur about them? Poor souls. I supposed they didn't. But I didn't blame them.

One day they would tell stories to their children and, if they were lucky, to their colleagues and students. "I was with him at the beginning," they would say. "And we could always tell. He had an air about him. The rest of us were apprehensive, but he stayed calm. It's as though he always knew the answer. Even then we could tell that he was great."

No one was watching me. I took out my pencil. The newly sharpened point had broken off in my pocket, but I took out my spare. I was ready for action.

The teacher arrived, a tall, balding man with an air of command. He would keep the others up to snuff. I would not be dragged down.

When he called the roll, my name was third. When it rang out, no one stirred, but surely those echoes I heard were not illusory. Even then, the building resounded with my presence.

After the roster was completed, the instructor offered a few directions about how the course would proceed. I barely listened, for I was pondering relativity. I could not worry about the schedule of quizzes.

With routine matters dispensed, the instructor indicated that first we would learn to use the slide rule. I concurred. The process would be annoying, but science could not be all glamour. Above the chalkboard was a giant demonstration model.

"Let's try something simple," he suggested. I agreed once more. After all, the other kids deserved a chance.

"Three times two. Focus the middle slat here on two. Slide the plastic cover over. There's your result. Six. Everybody clear? Good. Let's go on."

I hadn't quite managed to focus my middle slat.

"Let's try another. Six point seven times twenty-two. Slide this over, focus, measure up. Everybody have it?"

Three times two . . .

"Now let's try something more challenging. Point oh-seven times eight to the seventh power. Focus here. Slide this slat over there. And don't forget to align properly. Everybody okay?"

Three times two equals . . . seventy-four . . .

"Good enough. Let's get going. The first subject of the term will be motion. Force and velocity. The essential stuff of physics."

Three times two equals . . .

I put away the slide rule. They must have people in labs to do that kind of work. I was meant for bigger things.

The previous evening I had resolved to take notes in one book, then recopy them neatly in another. That way each night I could simultaneously synthesize the day's work and systematize my knowledge. Very scientific. Moreover, my biographer would have sufficient material to follow my development.

The class moved swiftly. I confessed inwardly that I did not understand precisely what was happening, but I consoled myself that when I regrouped that night, all would be under control. Even Einstein tended to learn slowly, as everyone knew.

At eight o'clock, I sat down at my dormitory room desk to solve the seven problems assigned for the following day. Before embarking on those, however, I opened my spiral and prepared to recopy the day's notes.

All I saw was a maze of letters, numbers, and arrows. Initially I imagined that for some reason I had kept writing my own name, but eventually I realized that the word I found six times was not "Victor," but "vector." Later I found several instances each of "force," "velocity," and "distance." At one o'clock I found a "time."

As I went to bed, a quiver of panic worked through my stomach. My only hope was that no one had been able to solve any of the problems, that our instructor had overestimated the abilities of his students.

The next morning I learned the truth: the weakest in the group had solved only five.

After class, I walked up to the teacher and explained that the solutions to the previous night's problems had not been completely clear. He moved to the board and talked for a few minutes. He drew some arrows, and he said "vector," "force," "distance," "velocity," and "time."

I nodded and left the room.

The next day we held our first lab, in which we were expected to study blocks of wood moving up and down inclined planes. Again, "vector," "force," and "velocity." Someone added "weight." The instructions were clear: "Turn in a report tomorrow." It was to be accompanied by a graph that showed how heavy the blocks became, or didn't become, as they went somewhere at some speed that might change if the blocks were heavier than the angle of the wood.

Or something like that.

My blocks didn't go anywhere.

Everyone else's graph was a gentle hill, sloping up, then down. Mine was rather like a corkscrew.

The first examination came on Friday. I wrote "distance" twice, then "velocity," "force," and "time." I drew some arrows, and I wrote some numbers. At the last minute, after I wrote my name on the answer sheet, I remembered to write "vector."

I earned a seven. Out of a hundred.

It was a gift seven.

On Saturday morning I transferred into French.

It was not much fun, as everyone spoke another language. Nevertheless, I understood more than I had in physics.

Perhaps I had aimed too high. People do that, of course. My talents lay elsewhere. Occasionally we must accept our limitations.

"I'd like this answer in cahns, please. Strictly in cahns."

That still has a wonderful ring.

Earlier versions of this material appeared the *The Phillips Exeter Bulletin* (Sept./Oct. 1979) and in my book *Classroom Virtuoso: Recollections of a Life in Learning* (Rowman & Littlefield, 2009). It is reprinted with permission, Copyright 1979, by the Trustees of Phillips Exeter Academy.

STEVEN M. CAHN is professor of philosophy at The City University of New York Graduate Center, where he served for nearly a decade as Provost and Vice President for Academic Affairs, then as Acting President.

He was born in Springfield, Massachusetts, in 1942, and earned his A.B. from Columbia College in 1963 and his Ph.D. in philosophy from Columbia University in 1966. He taught at Dartmouth College, Vassar College, New York University, the University of Rochester, and at the University of Vermont, where he chaired the Department of Philosophy.

He served as a program officer at the Exxon Education Foundation, as Acting Director for Humanities at The Rockefeller Foundation, and as the first Director of General Programs at the National Endowment for the Humanities. He formerly chaired the American Philosophical Association's Committee on the Teaching of Philosophy, was the Association's Delegate to the American Council of Learned Societies, and has been longtime President of The John Dewey Foundation.

Dr. Cahn is the author of ten books, including *Fate, Logic, and Time*; *The Eclipse of Excellence*; *Education and the Democratic Ideal*; *Puzzles & Perplexities: Collected Essays*; *God, Reason, and Religion*; *Saints and Scamps: Ethics in Academia*; and *From Student to Scholar: A Candid Guide to Becoming a Professor* (Columbia University Press).

He has edited or coedited some forty books, including *Moral Problems in Higher Education*; *Political Philosophy: The Essential Texts*, now in its second edition; *Exploring Philosophy: An Introductory Anthology*, now in its fourth edition; *Ethics: History, Theory, and Contemporary Issues*, now in its fifth edition; and *Classics of Western Philosophy*, now in its eighth edition.

Dr. Cahn has also served as general editor of four multivolume series: *Blackwell Philosophy Guides*; *Blackwell Readings in Philosophy*, *Issues in Academic Ethics*; and *Critical Essays on the Classics*.

His numerous articles have appeared in a broad spectrum of publications, including *The Journal of Philosophy*, *The Chronicle of Higher Education*, *Shakespeare Quarterly*, *The American Journal of Medicine*, *The New Republic*, and *The New York Times*.

A collection of essays written in his honor, edited by two of his former doctoral students, Robert B. Talisse of Vanderbilt University and Maureen Eckert of the University of Massachusetts Dartmouth, is titled *A Teacher's Life: Essays for Steven M. Cahn*.

Dr. Cahn lives in Old Greenwich, Connecticut, with his wife, Marilyn Ross, M.D.

VICTOR L. CAHN is professor of English at Skidmore College, where he teaches courses in Shakespeare, modern drama, history of drama, and expository writing.

He was born in New York City in 1948, and received his A.B. from Columbia College in 1969 and his M.A. (1973) and Ph.D. in English (1976) from New York University. He taught at Mercersburg Academy, Pomfret School, Phillips Exeter Academy, and Bowdoin College, and was recently profiled in *300 Best Professors* (edited by *The Princeton Review* and published by Random House).

He has written numerous books, including *Shakespeare the Playwright: A Companion to the Complete Tragedies, Histories, Comedies, and Romances* (named an Outstanding Academic Book by *Choice*); *The*

Plays of Shakespeare: A Thematic Guide; Political Animal: An Essay on Shakespeare's Henry V; Bard Games: The Shakespeare Quiz Book; Beyond Absurdity: The Plays of Tom Stoppard; Gender and Power in the Plays of Harold Pinter; Conquering College: A Guide for Undergraduates; the memoir *Classroom Virtuoso: Recollections of a Life in Learning*; and two novels, *Romantic Trapezoid* and *Sound Bites*.

His articles and reviews have appeared in such diverse publications as *Modern Drama, The Literary Review, The Chronicle of Higher Education, The New York Times,* and *Variety*.

Dr. Cahn is the author of many plays, several of which have been produced Off-Broadway as well as regionally: *Roses in December, Embraceable Me, Fit to Kill* (all published by Samuel French), *Getting the Business, Dally with the Devil, Sheepskin/Bottom of the Ninth,* and *Sherlock Solo*, a one-man show that he performs. He has also taken leading roles with theaters throughout the Capital Region of New York, in works by Shakespeare, Shaw, Pinter, Coward, Simon, Gurney, and Knott.

His primary avocation is the violin, and he has appeared as soloist both with orchestra and in recital with his brother, Steven M. Cahn.

Dr. Cahn lives in Saratoga Springs, NY.